Geraldine's years of wisdom shines from cover to cover. Her insights inspire ten times deeper connections with both prospects and current clientele in an industry where the journey of relationship building is just as important as the world we help others travel.
Vicki L. Freed, CTC – SVP, Sales at Royal Caribbean International

10X My Travel Business is a powerful resource for Travel Advisors navigating the post-pandemic world. Geraldine provides an accessible playbook and action plan to grow any travel business, including systems to capture and nurture the right customers. This is an important read at any stage of your business.
David Chait, Founder & CEO, Travefy

This is a must-read book for travel industry Leaders, Managers and Travel Advisors. Anyone in the post-COVID travel industry who feels like they are "hitting the wall" rebuilding and reinventing their business needs to read it. It offers useful and practical strategies built on Geraldine's wide experience in the industry. She gives a unique and timely perspective on how we can recover and thrive in the new business reality. I read the book in one sitting, and it sparked the first real excitement I have felt about my business in a long, long time.
Jeremy McLead, Expedia Cruises Franchise Owner, Victoria, BC

You nailed it! ... Very few people can capture my attention like Geraldine. Her business insight, combined with a unique ability to delve into the heart of meaningful topics for tomorrow's successful travel advisor, inspired me in this book.

Stéphanie Bishop, Managing Director, Globus Family of Brands

She leads the reader to discover ways to invest in yourself and build your business. The pandemic has made us rethink everything we know about business, and the travel industry has been hit harder than most. Geraldine Ree's 10X approach is a practical and useful guide for rethinking this NEW world of work - and she respectfully challenges us not to fall back into the habits of old. This book gets you thinking outside the box, about all the wonderful things that are possible in a post-pandemic world, and provides the strategies to achieve these goals.

Dr Selena Fisk, Data Storyteller

If you want a travel business that is highly profitable, meaningful and fulfilling, filled with clients that you love, Geraldine's 10X Your Business is the book for you! 10X My Travel Business is packed with unique insights, practical tips and actionable strategies for building a travel business that reflects your unique purpose and vision. There simply are no other training and sales tools available for travel agents that even come close to the level and quality of the information offered in this book.

Amanda Cummings, Travel Consultant

10X My Travel Business is a must-read for Travel Agency Owners and Advisors looking for a high-impact transformation. Geraldine's insight and experience draw you into a thought-provoking journey as to "why" you are in this business while uncovering the 10X framework for a successful rebuild in today's environment.

Janice Strand, Expedia Cruises Franchise Owner, Victoria BC

Geraldine drives home that 10X is about getting better, not working harder. Being better can be different for every individual travel professional; this isn't a one size fits all. It challenges every travel professional or travel leader to determine what they want their future to be, and set goals. She addresses the strife and challenges this industry has endured these past two years, the past is the past, and we can't change that. If you are still in the travel industry, this book is for you. Imagine finding a way to earn 10x more and work less; yes, it is possible.

Rhonda Stanley, CTA CTC, VP Talent Development,
The Travel Agent Next Door

Book design and layout: Sadie Butterworth-Jones
Editing by Mish Phillips and Emily Stephenson

For information about this title, please contact:
Geraldine Ree
www.geraldineree.com

Paperback ISBN 978-1-7775848-4-9
eBook ISBN 978-1-7775848-5-6

MY TRAVEL BUSINESS

Ten Times Better
in Half the Time

Geraldine Ree

My Dedication to the Silver Lining

This book is dedicated to the silver lining that has carried the travel industry through the pandemic.

This silver lining, like all silver linings, is only possible because of the setback.

The past two years have been a life lesson in what it means to be resilient.

I've come to realize that resilience isn't a coat of armour. It's not a temporary fix for a single obstacle. Nor is it simply hanging on through tough times and hoping for the best.

Resilience means to keep moving forward with an attitude of optimism that no matter what is happening around you, there is value in what each moment teaches you.

What you learn from the moment, no matter how difficult, makes the next one easier.

Today's tough announcement, or yesterday's cancellation, make tomorrow's news much easier to rally around. Even though Lucy keeps moving the ball, there is always a way to move it forward.

Your ability to navigate unprecedented uncertainty, to rise above it and respond with a whole new level of agility has been remarkable.

It's these actions that have redefined resilience and have become the industry's collective silver lining.

We are stronger, better, and more resilient than ever.

It is my deepest hope that the lessons of the past two years will bring you hope, abundance and joy now and in your future.

Acknowledgements

To my husband, Cam, I am forever grateful for your love, support, and tireless proofreading! Without you, I would never be where I am or who I am today. You are my shining example of what it means to never, ever give up!

To my family, keep living your faith and generously sharing your remarkable gifts with the world.

Contents

My Dedication to the Silver Lining vii

Acknowledgements ix

Introduction: Are You 10X Ready? 13

Part One: What Is 10X? 27

    Chapter 1: The 10X Way of Thinking 31

    Chapter 2: The 10X Lens 41

Part Two: How 10X Works 63

    Chapter 3: The 10X Framework 65

Part Three: The Four 10X Strategies 87

    Chapter 4: 10X Connection:
    Connection Is Currency 89

Chapter 5: 10X Conversion:
The Art of Creating High Value Customers 115

Chapter 6: 10X Commerce:
Earn More Money in Less Time 135

Chapter 7: 10X Impact — Part One:
Making a Difference: To be Transformational is Priceless 169

Chapter 8: 10X Impact — Part Two:
Executing the Dream 215

Part Four: 10X Leadership 247

Chapter 9: 10X Together: How to Engage
a Superstar Team and Retain High Performers 249

Conclusion 271

About Geraldine Ree 279

Connect With Me 281

Introduction
Are You 10X Ready?

The answer to that seems obvious.

I am more than ready! Wait, what is the question?

The question is, are you ready to come back bigger, better, and bolder than you were pre-pandemic?

This book is about creating a high-impact transformation of your travel business.

You might ask, "Which business are you referring to: the one I have now, or the one I had going into 2020?

That is a fair question.

Where do you start a transformation when the business you've known, possibly for years, doesn't look anything like it ever did before?

The business as you knew it does not exist anymore.

Consider salmon returning home to spawn. When they finally lay their eggs, they will grow their species, not 10 times, not 100 times but 2500 times the size once they reach their spawning ground.

Salmon face a lot of obstacles during the salmon run. For starters, they have to swim against the river's current the whole way; sometimes up to 4,000 kilometres!

Salmon also leap over waterfalls, rapids, and dams. Believe it or not, these amazing fish can jump two meters high. They also have skilled predators like bears and eagles who wait around every river bend to catch them when they jump out of the water.

Growing your travel business coming out of Covid is like swimming hard upstream. You are jumping high to learn new Covid rules, and dodging predators such as like emerging wars and travel-shamers.

However, unlike salmon, which can find their way home after years away, you cannot return to where you were before.

Returning to your original travel business is like completing a long and arduous swim only to find out you're in the wrong stream.

The purpose of this book is to clarify which stream you are swimming in. It will help you find a stream based on your new passions and new consumer demand; one that allows you to showcase your unique gifts and abilities.

Finally, a stream that allows you to be your best self, doing work you love, with people you love working with.

The brutal truth (and silver lining) is that your new stream contains the pandemic.

We are never going to have a Covid-free world again. Even if the virus is contained, there may be new strains, changes to travel advisories, and other forms of adversity. Global warming is pressing on the heels of the pandemic and packs significant consequences for humanity now and in the future. The war between Russia and Ukraine seems surreal after such a global awakening to the need for love and compassion. It has generated untold losses of life and property, with millions of people forcibly displaced. It truly is tragic.

The silver lining is that travel — and the light it can bring into the world — has not wavered. Our ability to spend time with people we care about and have life-changing experiences has never felt more valuable. The demand for travel is on the rise with record-breaking numbers of future bookings. World cruises are selling out within hours. Luxury travel is the fastest growing segment. People are willing to pay for privacy and additional layers of safety such as having fewer guests and more space.

People are beginning to come to terms with traveling with some degree of risk. This book faces the realities of navigating Covid and the challenges within your new stream. It also explores the massive opportunity of a post-pandemic travel business.

I truly believe that the comeback is not better than the setback. The comeback is IN the setback.

The goal of this book is to help you grow your business to new heights that are only possible because you are in the new stream.

Is the new stream easier or harder than the old stream? That depends on your perspective and approach.

It's not about swimming harder. It's about finding a way to think bigger and to find better ways of doing things. It's about creating more joy and finding better clients in less time. It's about raising your game.

By the time you finish reading this book, you'll have everything you need to navigate the new stream and to find new insights on the skills which will serve you well in the new travel era.

The Problems We Are Solving

Problem #1: You've become a travel operator.
"Can I pick your brain?"

When I was fresh out of high school, I became an operator for BC Tel. It was the best job in the world for getting a birds-eye view of human problem-solving.

In those days, long before bots and chats were a thing, anyone in the world could pick up a phone and dial "zero". And boy, they did!

As you might expect, queries were most often about calling people. However, over those phones I experienced everything from witnessing a marriage proposals to helping someone fight for their life, and it's strange how often people called wanting to know the correct time!

It is human nature to take the path of least resistance. What's the quickest way to get answers?

Travel's version of calling the operator is calling you for answers about Covid and travel. You are the path of least resistance to a human voice.

According to Answer the Public, in February 2022 there were over 225 billion searches on travel and Covid.

- Are Covid tests free?

- What are the rules for Covid and travel?

- Where can I travel with Covid?

- What insurance am I eligible for with travel and Covid?

- And so on!

Suddenly, advisors find themselves in the crossfire of these Google searches.

When people need to make decisions about travel, whether they've booked with you or not, a number of these 225 billion searches find their way to a travel advisor.

The problem is not just how we answer the queries. It's how we respond in a way that makes us feel joyful, rather than drained. Just look at Facebook for the occasional rant from the advisor who's had their brain picked one too many times — ouch!

So, how do we incorporate these questions into our business model so that they become opportunities?

Problem #2: Finding a steady flow of high-quality leads.

You have cancelled and rebooked so often that you're tempted to sit it out for a while until things get back to "normal". Who could blame you? This has not been easy. However, deep down you know that getting out of the game is not the best option.

The challenge is finding clients who have a travel resilience factor that you can work with.

Covid has removed the predictability you've grown accustomed to. Pre-pandemic, people — especially those of a certain age — would travel every one or two years and follow fairly predictable travel patterns. You could count on an empty nester to plan at least three bucket-list trips upon or just after retirement.

Now, those who travel frequently may be among the segment that wants to wait until the pandemic is "over".

You can do the research, find the best vacation and add the right insurance. However, if a customer isn't ready or their spouse isn't ready, your work will be relegated to the perpetual do-over pile. Meanwhile, others less known to you are asking where they can go as soon as possible.

Finding a steady stream of high-end clients has become an extraordinary challenge.

Problem #3: Too much work for the money, travel perks, and time off.

Prior to the pandemic, you were ready to switch to higher-end travel. You longed for a more discerning customer. You were tired of the price shoppers and the tyre kickers.

In 2019, when doing the research for my first book, *Flying Colours*, I interviewed hundreds of travel advisors. When asked, "What are the biggest challenges you are facing?", these were the top two responses:

1.   Not enough high-end clients.

2.   Too much work for the money.

This book is intended to get you earning more and having better clients. However, the problem is not what you think.

It's not the size of the market, the travel protocols, the supplier commissions, or the lack of support, though those may all play a role.

The real problem is that the layers of cancellations, complexity and new consumer demands are stretching you to breaking point. Take away your pay, your time off, and your personal travel, and suddenly it all snaps.

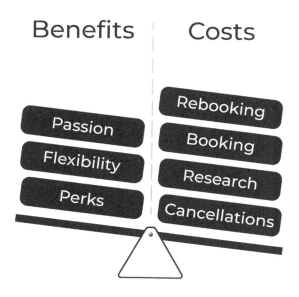

"There's a difference between giving up and knowing when you've had enough."

~ Author unknown

To get the cost-benefit scale to balance, you need to find highly motivating reasons to stay. You need to decide on what is your own personal motivation.

It's not just the passion, perks, or the flexibility.

Balancing the scale requires three key elements to come into play.

First, acknowledge what it took for you to stay. You've shown a kind of resilience that few outside our industry would understand.

Something much deeper within you called you to stay. Tapping into your resilience of purpose is going to be a secret weapon for you going forward.

Next, the unprecedented pent-up demand will, at least for a period of time, sustain you. Consumers are making up for lost time by booking longer, more expensive trips.

Your pipeline will have a steady stream of high value clients, as long as you know how to access it.

Lastly, tipping the scale in your favour comes down to finding new capacity to do more things in less time. That's the 10X factor that we will reveal in this book.

It's time to find a new stream.

Chapter Summary
Are You 10X Ready?

- This book is about a high-impact transformation of your travel business.

- The challenge with looking back is that the business you had doesn't exist anymore.

- Travel is on the rise; there is an unprecedented demand for future travel.

- Advisors are caught in the crossfire of Google searches for answers to the questions of Covid and travel.

- Finding a steady stream of high-end clients has become the ultimate challenge.

- The real problem is that the layers of cancellations, complexity and new consumer demands are stretching you to breaking point.

- Something much deeper within you is calling you to stay. Only when you can tap into that higher purpose will you discover the ability to tip the scale right over to the other side.

Points to Ponder

- Looking back, why did you start your travel business in the first place?

- Which of those reasons still exist today?

- What is the pandemic teaching you about your travel business?

- What scares you the most about staying in the travel business?

- Why did you decide to stay in the travel business?

- How will you leverage your internal motivation to succeed after all you've endured?

Part One

What Is 10X?

The 10X Way of Thinking

You might be wondering what exactly 10X is and how it applies to your travel business.

The purpose of a 10X goal is to breathe new life into your old way of doing things.

On the surface, what is a travel business? It's selling travel throughout the world to a list of customers. It requires sales, marketing, technology, product knowledge, and most of all, your passion and commitment to excellence.

That has not changed.

The challenge is that while the basic model of a travel business hasn't changed, everything else has.

The world is different now. Beyond the obvious safety protocols, humanity has shifted. The purpose and meaning behind travel has grown.

If we're not careful, it would be easy to fall into our old ways of doing business.

If you want to comeback better, you need to set a higher bar for yourself.

Aspiring to grow your business 1OX, or ten times better in half the time, is a gigantic leap. It may sound dramatic, and it is for good reason.

It will create the kind of paradigm shift you need to acknowledge you're in a new, different, and far better stream.

Why Does It Matter?

You've stayed this long, endured incredible hardship, and now I'm asking you to consider a 1OX approach.

Why does it matter if you stay and do the work?

It matters because you matter. Sharing your unique passion for travel is something that lights you up and makes a difference to you and everyone around you.

It matters because there is an unprecedented opportunity ahead to build a much more lucrative travel business. The average spend, frequency of travel, and the demand for modern luxury travel are all in your favour.

It matters because you're needed.

- **Suppliers need you.** You are the trusted voice of thousands of hotels, cruise beds, tour operators, and other hospitality channels.

- **Host agencies and consortia need you.** You are at the core of their business model and without you proactively growing your business, they are not able to get the support they need and give you what you need.

- **Travelers need you because they have questions.** They have 250 billion questions and they are better off relying on a single trusted source for their answers.

All of these sectors of the industry depend on you. It's estimated that 30% of advisors have left the industry. Some may return when cash flow is more predictable, while others have retired or left permanently.

I could go on with a long list of reasons for growing your travel business.

However, unless you believe that the travel industry is where you belong and where you want to make a difference, then it doesn't really matter.

The pre-pandemic world of travel had plenty of room for people who never had to think about the tug of war between the amount of work and the benefits because the benefits always won.

The new world we are faced with is one where you need to make the choice to stay. There is no room for halfway committed when you consider the steep climb ahead.

I highly recommend reading Seth Godin's book, *The Dip*. He emphasizes that every entrepreneur faces a dip. He argues that it's okay to quit; there is no shame in leaving something that no longer works for you.

However, if you stay, prepare yourself to be "Best in the world".

"To be a superstar, you must do something exceptional. Not just survive the Dip, but use the Dip as an opportunity to create something so extraordinary that people can't help but talk about it, recommend it, and, yes, choose it."

It's going to take work to be the best.

You're going to do the work anyway, so let me explain why 10X goals will set you up for success beyond what you ever thought possible.

Chapter 1
The 10X Way of Thinking

I've always been a big goal-setter. I grew up as a competitive figure skater. Setting goals to get to the next level was instilled in me at a very early age.

The climb up the figure skating ladder is a measured one. Skaters are required to progress through badges, figures, and dance levels from bronze to silver to gold.

Pianists practise their scales, singers their octaves and skaters their crossovers. Doing the work is directly tied to getting a better result.

The goal for most skaters, pianists, or singers, is to get to the next level, one step at a time.

Yet there were those rare skaters who, from the moment they breezed by me, jumped higher, spun faster, and flew through the levels.

They had desire in their bellies, and their skates were on fire. They had their eye on a bigger prize such as winning local events, Nationals or even Olympic medals.

As I look back now, I wonder if they jumped higher, with that big goal in mind. Could the idea of winning a gold medal be enough to raise their game early on?

I'd also been surrounded by visionaries. The founder of Expedia Cruises, Michael Drever is one of the brightest visionaries I have ever met. He could rapture an entire room on the back of a cocktail napkin. His ability not just to see the future, but to shine the light for others to see it too, was remarkable.

Was he born a visionary? There is no doubt he is gifted. How did his desire to create the largest cruise-only organization in the world fuel his ability to rapture the room?

As I began putting the pieces of goalsetting together, these questions started to shape the idea of 10X thinking. The idea is that what we think and dream about for the future directly impacts what we choose to do each day. In fact, the more compelling the dream, the more likely we are to practise our scales or to engage the people around us in our vision.

In short, we are highly motivated to get better because better always precedes bigger.

What I learned is that 10X thinking is the first step in goal *getting*. In fact, thinking bigger is the single most important difference between *setting* and *getting* goals.

If the vision isn't big enough or compelling enough, you simply will not be motivated to do the work.

However, 10X thinking is only a small element of the bigger picture of *10X My Travel Business*.

If you're like me, you need more evidence to buy in. I get it.

I am a practical enthusiast. I am the first one to jump on board with a vision, as long as I'm given enough data and evidence to protect me from making the wrong decision.

Let's start by exploring two of the prominent thought leaders on 10X thinking.

The 10X Mindset — Dan Sullivan

Dan Sullivan is a leadership expert and world-renowned entrepreneur coach. He explains why setting your sights on 10X is easier than growing by 2X.

The reason Dan Sullivan recommends expressing your goal by 10x rather than anything less is compelling.

"When you set your sights on the goal of a 10x bigger future, something immediately happens to your thinking, your innovation, your decision-making, your communication, and your action."
~ Dan Sullivan

According to Sullivan, incremental goals (like 2x) simply don't engage people the same way intellectually or emotionally.

I believe he is right — setting 10X goals by dreaming 10X bigger sets your creativity and inspiration in motion.

The fine print, however, is that you must commit to the 10X goal.

I believe that thinking bigger is important. But everything you need to do to commit to the 10X goal cannot be understated. Setting the 10X goal without committing to the smaller actions is almost worse than not setting the goal in the first place.

When you skip the steps necessary to commit to the goal, you end up defeated and somewhat reluctant to ever set goals again. How many of us hate setting new years' resolutions because of our past track record?

For the past twenty years, I've worked on my own version of 10X goalsetting. I have a long list of goals that have come true years after setting them in motion. I've also got more than my fair share of dreaming and scheming ideas that failed to get off the ground.

When my daughter was born, my best friend and I thought about starting a diaper business. The thought of it now makes me laugh out loud.

I agree with Dan Sullivan that a 10X goal creates excitement and motivation. A vision for your goal that is fully manifested in your mind has compelling energy.

However, in light of the pandemic, when the rug has been pulled out from underneath you on multiple occasions, it seems counter-intuitive to consider a 10X goal when all you can think about is treading water.

More and more, I hear agency owners and advisors saying, "I'll be happy just to get where I was".

You can hear the anxiety in their voices. It's hard to imagine they will have the inspiration they need to keep working towards their goal when the going gets tough.

So, knowing the steep mountain ahead that we need to climb just to reach our former altitude, what is the solution?

We must move away from the idea of getting back to where we were. We can't go back to the same stream. Instead, light up your imagination with a 10X goal for your comeback. Then, hold that thought. For the rest of the book, we will uncover what it takes to commit to that goal.

First, let's consider a second thought leader on 10X thinking: Grant Cardone.

The 10X Rule — Grant Cardone

In his book, *The 10X Rule*, Grant Cardone holds firmly to the truth that world domination only exists when you are willing to work 10 times harder than others are willing to.

> *"This is the focus of the 10X Rule:*
> *You must set targets that are 10X what you think*
> *you want and then do 10 times what you think*
> *it will taketo accomplish those targets. Massive*
> *thoughts must be followed by massive actions."*
> *~ Grant Cardone*

I agree with Grant. The actions you take to achieve your 10X goals must be massive. It's like jumping into a cold lake. Almost by instinct, you move your arms and legs vigorously to warm up your body and fight off the cold.

However, they need to be the right actions. It also can't be such a massive action that it's not sustainable.

The one thing I know for sure is that 10X cannot mean ten times more wasted work. You've been through too much to invest massive effort without a solid plan with clear boundaries in place.

I frequently ask travel advisors to imagine their business 10X bigger. The response is usually the same.

Can you achieve it? "Yes, probably."

Do you want to achieve it? *"No, I don't want to work that hard."*

Do not assume the incorrect conclusion that 10X thinking means it will take ten times the work. There is a way to grow by 10X without working any harder. In fact, you will work less when you find a better way.

We know that working harder alone is not the solution. When exhaustion sets in, emotions run high. Your body creates a chemical reaction to the adrenaline and you lose productivity. Over time, this leads to serious health implications, even death.

According to the World Health Organization:

> *"Working 55 hours or more per week is a serious health hazard. It's time that we all, governments, employers, and employees wake up to the fact that long working hours can lead to premature death."*

The 10X My Travel Business Approach by Geraldine Ree

Now that we've considered Dan Sullivan and Grant Cardone's version of 10X thinking, we can connect their timeless principles with the unique battles you are facing in the travel industry.

We know that your current stream demands too much work for the money. You lack a steady flow of high-end leads. You face continuous uncertainty, and the new burden of responsibility.

Working harder is not the answer. Setting big goals seems like a guessing game with so many unknowns ahead of you.

Yet, thinking bigger, in all its glory, is essential.

It's about reimagining what your travel business could be and taking the right actions to propel your business forward. It does not mean more work. It means a bigger vision combined with the right work.

The 10X My Travel Business solution helps you become ten times *better* in every area of your business. Ten times better at finding and keeping good clients, better at being commercially smart, better at pacing yourself, and better at saying no.

- Yes, you need to think bigger — think as big as you can!

- Yes, you need to work harder. But harder at the right things such as finding joy in the work itself.

- Yes, you need to stop doing things that don't add a single customer to your business.

It is possible to earn ten times more and work less. I realize that may sound extreme. Trust me, I had my doubts. However, after seeing firsthand, top people in their field who have implemented this 10X approach of thinking big, continuously getting better, and setting rigorous boundaries about what NOT to do, I firmly believe that this approach works.

Your version of getting ten times better might be to create a business you can work from anywhere. It might be to earn enough to fund your personal travel or to only sell a certain style of travel. Or it might be to earn six figures without working 80 hours a week.

In his book, *Company of One, Why Staying Small is the Next Big Thing in Business*, Paul Jarvis writes,

"The point of business, at least why I love people getting into business, is because they want more freedom in their lives."

Like it is for most travel agents, travel is part of your freedom and a key part of your compensation package. One of the reasons the pandemic has been so hard on you is that you haven't earned your commission or enjoyed your travel benefits.

The 10X approach will help you get there again, in a bigger way than you could even imagine for yourself.

At the very least, you will learn to think bigger whilst doing less. Initially, you'll find small ways to pick up speed, without the drag of "busy work" slowing you down.

At most, after reading this book and putting the ideas into practice, you will set a 10X goal for yourself and find yourself better off in every way that matters.

Chapter 2
The 10X Lens

Every day is a new day; a chance to create something remarkable. It's also a chance to fritter away your time and energy.

Days cumulate to become weeks, weeks become months and months become years. The choice is yours: become continually better or perpetually farther behind.

A 10X lens provides a bird's-eye view of your business that helps keep you on track so that you are building towards a bigger future, rather than losing ground.

Think of a day as a container that can hold limited time and energy. The best way to determine what comes out of the container is to be very thoughtful about what goes in.

- Your actions are selected in terms of their impact on your goals. Those are your ingredients.

- You mix in a way that creates the right consistency. That is your process.

- The outcome improves by the combination of what you put in, and how you mix it. That is your result.

10X results don't appear in a day, but are a daily endeavour.

The 10X lens is a daily starting point for achieving your goals. No matter what point you are at in your journey, you can use this lens as a compass for direction, a benchmark for progress, and a tool for making good decisions.

Let's examine this lens in more detail.

10X
READY
Capacity

Eliminate   AIM   Initiate

FIRE
Capability

The 10X lens has three stages: Ready, Aim, Fire! The goal is to move up the lens from having the capacity to grow, to the capability to grow. Along the way, you'll need a strategy for choosing your actions.

1 **Capacity** — Ready

2 **Yes** — Initiate — Aim

(3)   **No** — Eliminate — Aim

(4)   **Capability** — Fire

Let's review each of these.

Capacity — Are You 10X Ready?

Begin your 10X journey by examining your capacity. All growth requires a new effort that competes for your time and energy. If your container is full, something must give.

My mother-in-law taught me how to cook 15 years before I met her son. She was my eighth grade home economics teacher. I'll never forget learning how to measure butter. You can't put butter directly into a measuring cup because it will stick to the walls, and you'll lose too much in the transfer.

You measure butter by filling a liquid measuring cup with half a cup of water. You put the butter into the water until it rises to a full cup. Magic! You now have exactly half a cup of butter.

If you were to put the butter into a full cup of water, it would overflow.

In the same way, the reason so many new goals fail is that we try to add them into a very full cup.

You could have the most exciting goals for your comeback. However, you must acknowledge the limits of your new container.

Booking travel takes longer now. There are excruciating hold times, changing rules, and details to be triple-checked.

You are also going to be a little rusty as it's been two long years since you had clients traveling. For the foreseeable future, travel advisors will need to make room for a new level of attention to detail on each booking.

To be 10X ready, you need to prepare to pour some things out of your cup to create capacity for the comeback.

The comeback is going to require more intentional time and energy.

Energy

First, let's consider how your energy creates additional capacity to make a 10X shift.

We are all born with a natural level of energy. Some people can't sit still, while others crave the horizontal position.

Neither are absolute, so the key is to understand your own level of energy.

I'm a morning person, but there is only one fresh start to each day, so I've become very creative in finding new ways to increase my energy so that I have a second burst of productivity in the afternoon.

Here are just a few ways you can hack a fresh start and increase energy levels:

1. Go for a brisk walk outside

2. Exercise

3. Take a nap

4. Meditate

5. Have a good laugh

6. Phone a friend

7. Watch an inspirational speaker

8. Switch rooms

9. Stand up

10. Spark joy by adding fun breaks into your calendar.

Time

Time is the most obvious limit to your capacity. Unfortunately, you cannot create more time.

The interesting thing about time limits is that they often improve your productivity. Think about how productive you are the day before you go on vacation! You push things through at lightning speed, knowing there is a beach at the other end of your hard work.

The only way to increase your capacity in time is to use it wisely.

There are three ways to use time more effectively.

First, remove every item in your container that competes for your time if it is not as effective as other choices.

Second is to track time, and set limits to your need to be perfect. One of the biggest time stealers is working to the point of perfection when "good enough" would do.

Last, learn to leverage your time. Do it once, and use it often. With every single thing you do, consider how else you could use this effort. We'll explore this concept more in later chapters.

Clearly, it's how you spend your time that determines the output of your business.

Capacity is a combination of having the time and energy to do the right things.

Aim — A Yes or No Decision

As we move up the 10X lens from capacity to capability, you'll see the left- and right-hand side of the model marked 'Yes — Initiate', and 'No — Eliminate'.

The reason many people never move up from capacity to capability is fear. Fear is the biggest thief of your time. What if I fail? What if this is too hard? Why did I do that? That will never work. Who am I to want this for myself?

According to the National Science Foundation, the average person has 12,000 to 60,000 thoughts per day. Of those, 80 per cent are negative and 95 per cent are repetitive.

These repetitive, negative questions fill you with fear and prevent you from asking the most important question of all.

What should I do next?

In order to achieve everything I want from this day, this week, this year, you only have to know and do one thing. You must know your next move — and take it!

The 10X lens is designed to take into consideration all the possibilities of the moment.

If you've been stuck on the same level for a long time, consider what is holding you back from starting something new.

In order to move from capacity to capability, you need new skills. It requires a yes or no decision as to whether your next move will take you closer to your 10X goal.

Yes or No?

Yes, I will do this today; no, I will not do this today.

A meaningless yes looks like this: yes. It's a flat yes with no conditions that leaves you wide open to procrastination or failure. An enthusiastic yes has a metaphorical (and a literal) "s".

My mother used to push back if she ever heard a "ya" in our house.

It wasn't just the grammatical slang that she objected to. Yes with an "s" shows that you are fully committed to doing the work!

Saying yes well looks like this:

- Yes, this will be a concrete step towards my goal.

- Yes, doing this today will help me grow.

- Yes, doing this today will save me time.

- Yes, doing this today will make me money.

Deciding what you say yes to must be somehow linked to improving the likelihood of achieving your long-term goal.

On the other hand, saying no may be even more valuable, especially when that is hard for you.

When asked how he created the statue of David, Michelangelo shared, "I chip away at everything that isn't David".

The impact of saying no can be profound.

Saying no with conviction looks like this:

- No, this is a distraction from my goal.

- No, nobody asked me to do this or needs me to do this.

- No, doing this today will not help my growth.

- No, doing this today will waste my time.

- No, doing this today won't earn me any more money.

So, how do you decide: yes, or no? It's not always a black-and-white decision.

Your decisions are based on your big goals and dreams. What you do in a day will be much like your decision on which route to take when traveling by car.

When you type a destination into Google Maps, it will often give you the fastest route and one or two alternatives.

Do you want to take the fastest route, the scenic route, or somewhere in between?

Often, you know things about the route that does not fit into any algorithm.

For example, normally you don't book air only for certain clients but, because of the pandemic, you've taken on every request.

You are coming to the point in your comeback where you need to make critical yes or no decisions about the type of business that works best for you.

Which direction do you want to take now that demand is booming?

A strategy is a "yes" or "no" checklist to achieve what you want, the way you want!

Let's dig in a little more to what each of these decisions means for growing your business.

YES — Initiate

Saying yes means you're going to initiate something new. New beginnings are very exciting!

Starting a new client relationship, goal, or chapter brings optimism to your business.

Starting your day strong with a sense of optimism can sustain your whole day. In in his book, *Miracle Morning*, Hal Elrod states:

"You win the morning, you win the day."

There are three keys to saying yes well.

 Understand all of your options.
Remember that client who complained to you about the flights you chose... until you showed him that it was the best of all possible options based on the time of year and other factors.

Take time to get everything out of your head.
Start with a mind map placing your big goal in the
centre. Radiate branches of ideas that will propel
you forward. Include all the big drivers such as
customers, sales, marketing, finance, administration,
and suppliers.

 **Do the one thing that matters most.**
The most important step in saying yes well is to
identify the most important next step. You don't have
to know every step towards your goal. You just have
to know the next step, and take it!

Gary Keller's book, *The One Thing,* asks:

> *"What's the ONE thing that I can do, such that by
> doing it, everything else is easier or unnecessary?"*

Match the yes with the time and energy available.
You are limited on time and resources for filling your
container, yet you tend to write arm-length to-do lists.

While it feels good to get it out on paper — and you must —
this is not the best strategy for planning your day.

The yes needs to be realistic given the time and energy you
have available. It's like a finer version of being 10X ready.
Are you fully ready for the yes?

For example, there are some projects that work well to chip away at for one hour here or even 15 minutes there. You can make great progress over time.

Others you want to say yes to but you know the best approach is to take a full day out of the "office". Quarterly planning for example. Every 90 days, you need to take time to work on your business.

No — Eliminate

The "stop doing" list.

When I was at Expedia Cruises, and similarly during my own business start-up, the list of ideas was endless. There were so many exciting projects to get your business fully off the ground.

Somewhere between *Go* and *Park Place*, you realize that you're still working in start-up mode. You need to start adding houses and hotels! You need to start making progress on the ideas that matter most to you.

A 'stop doing' list is a necessary part of your going — gold strategy. Below are just a few ideas of things that you can stop doing as your business grows.

From:	To:
Every supplier webinar	Key Partner replays at x1.25 speed
Social media throughout the day	Social media once per day for business-building
One-hour meetings	15-minute meetings
Ten emails	One phone call
Beating yourself up for errors	Win-or-learn mindset

Another reason that saying no is so important is that it is often easier in the moment to say yes. "Just this one time" is a sneaky lie we tell ourselves instead of taking time to stop doing things.

We get into deep patterns and routines and it is hard to give up things we do for things we could do better.

Yet, your container has limits. Whenever you start something, ask yourself what you are going to stop doing to make room for the new initiative.

This is another timeless lesson I learned growing up. We had a box at the end of the hall for our "gently used clothing". Every month, we would collect our deposits and take them to the local women's shelter.

When I was old enough to start buying my own clothes, my parents taught me that whenever I buy something new, to give the same number of articles away.

Start/stop, initiate/eliminate, east/west... it's the yin and yang of staying on track towards your goals.

Fire! Your Capability Sets You Apart

The last stage of the model is to move from capacity to capability by improving your ability to run and grow your travel business.

Human nature is to want to find the best. The best hairdresser, the best painter, the best doctor. Therefore, the most effective and lasting way to attract clients is to simply be the best.

When you are the best in the world, you are the go-to for all of the people who are looking for your unique experience, essence, and expertise.

People don't ask for mediocre movie recommendations. Even an average movie review is enough to dampen our enthusiasm to spend our precious time. We set our bar high, hoping for nothing below eight Rotten Tomatoes. Anything below 70 per cent loses its fresh designation.

In his book, *So Good They Can't Ignore You*, Cal Newport reveals an astonishing truth. He says, "Don't follow your passion" because doing so can lead us to unrealistic expectations of what our passion can do for us.

> *"If you want to love what you do, abandon the passion mindset (what can the world offer me?) and instead adopt the craftsman mindset (what can I offer the world?)"*

It's been an eye-opening experience through the pandemic to watch the travel industry, based almost entirely on passion, come to terms with what that means. When you strip away the excitement and obvious benefits of travel, you're left questioning why you're in the travel business.

More importantly, why you stay.

I believe that if you're still here, it's the latter (what can I offer the world?). Now it's time to invest in the quality of your work so that your dedication pays off. It's time to develop a craftsman attitude.

A craftsman invests in the skills of their craft until they become a master.

The direction of your business is determined by your goals. The trajectory of your business is determined by your craftsmanlike ability to deliver extraordinary experiences for travelers, every step along the way.

Your capability is what sets you apart from everyone else.

Capability lies in shifting from being all things to all people, to becoming indispensable to a finite list of ideal customers.

The reason you need such rigor around capacity, and discipline around your yes and no decisions is that capability is the game changer you are looking for.

Capability means getting better. When you get 10X better, everything else becomes easier or unnecessary.

Chapter Summary
10X Thinking and the 10X Lens

- Growing 10X matters because you matter. The opportunity ahead is unprecedented and growing in all the ways you need to create a 10X shift.

- You are needed! Suppliers need you, hosts and consortia need you, travelers need you!

- 10X thinking means that what we think and dream about for the future directly impacts what we choose to do each day.

- Incremental goals (like 2x) simply don't engage people the same way intellectually or emotionally.

- Massive thoughts must be followed by massive action.

- 10X thinking in the travel industry is about reimagining what your travel business could be and taking the right actions to propel your business forward.

- It does not mean more work. It means a bigger vision combined with the right work.

- A 10X lens is a bird's-eye view of your business that helps keep you on track so that you are building towards a bigger future rather than losing ground.

- The comeback is going to require a heightened sense of both time and energy.

- Your trajectory and speed always depend on the decisions you make along the way.

- Start/stop, yes/no and initiate/eliminate are the yin and yang of staying on track towards your goals.

- The trajectory of your business is determined by your craftsmanlike ability to deliver extraordinary experiences for travelers, every step along the way.

Points to Ponder

- How does what you think about impact your day?

- How might thinking about a bigger future motivate you to do something differently in the present?

- What are your deepest fears about thinking bigger?

- What is the worst thing that could happen if you acted on your big ideas for your travel business?

- How could you mitigate that risk?

- What does it mean to be 10X ready?

- What do you need to start doing differently?

- What do you need to stop doing?

- If you could be famous for one thing, what would it be?

- How would being famous for that impact your travel business?

Part Two

How 10X Works

Chapter 3
The 10X Framework

How to Apply 10X Thinking
to All Areas of Your Business

The secret to growing ten times better in half the time is continuity. It is about applying 10X thinking to every area of your business, rather than a bandaid solution to a single opportunity, problem area or roadblock.

Consider the foundation of a building. It's a combination of materials and structure. It's the first phase of building. It sets limits and boundaries to the size and scale of the building. It protects the building from outside forces and adverse conditions such as earthquakes and hurricanes.

Without a carefully constructed foundation, the building will crack and eventually crumble or collapse.

In the same way, if you set goals for your business without ensuring you have the right materials and structure, even the best intentions will falter. If you don't account for worst case scenarios, such as future pandemics, new skills required, or changes in your financial practices, there will be limits to your potential growth.

When I was a DSM for Princess Cruises, I decided my goal was to win DSM of the Year. I was going to grow each of my top 75 accounts by 30%. The calculator spit out a number that was so big I got very excited! I knew that it was more than enough to win the prize.

My plan was simple. I would host a cruise night with each of them in the first quarter of the year.

I enthusiastically shared my plans, which were met with great promise!

Soon after, I discovered my plan was flawed. Suddenly, my calendar had me doing 31 cruise events in 45 days. I realized it was not sustainable.

I had a 10X goal that was solely focused on getting bigger — fast!

Not every account needed or was ready for my "one size fits all" solution.

By putting the 10X framework in place, you can rebuild your travel business for the long haul.

The 10X framework is the foundation necessary for getting ten times better in half the time.

To 10X your business the right way, you need to focus on the four core areas of your business that, over time, will bring you the most of what you want. Whether it's more money, more freedom, more travel or more and better customers, the answer lies in these areas: purpose, people, process, and performance.

The 10X Framework

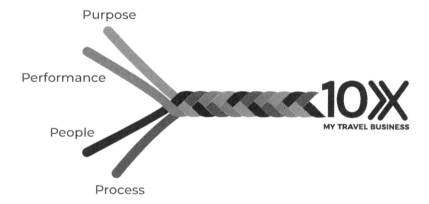

1. Purpose
How to stand out from the crowd.

Mark Twain said,

> *"The two most important days in your life are the day you are born and the day you find out why."*

The travel world is crowded with thousands of *passionate* advisors.

Check out any travel website (including my own!) and you're likely to find the word 'passion' or something similar in the 'About Me' section.

Passion is common to everyone — it's the lifeblood of our industry. Even travelers are passionate.

Your purpose, on the other hand, is completely unique to you.

It is, therefore, the ultimate competitive advantage.

By finding your purpose and communicating how important it is to your travel business, you will stand out. Nobody can do you as you can. Nobody does travel the way you do.

Finding your purpose starts with finding your "why". From Simon Sinek, we have learned that,

"People don't buy what you do; they buy why you do it."

Simon and many other thought leaders like him have helped an entire business community understand the importance of knowing their "why". If you have not already done so, I highly recommend his Ted Talk and book, *Finding Your Why*.

He helps the audience and reader understand how compelling their why is to their customer.

Let's take some time to look at your own why, and the role it plays in your travel business.

Why Did You Start Your Travel Business?

Let's go back to the day you decided to become a travel advisor. Why did you decide to join the industry?

Perhaps you were passionate about traveling the globe. Maybe you loved cruising, or finding those off-the-beaten-path getaways, and wanted to share your experiences with others so that they could experience the same joy.

These are all good reasons to be in this business. However, the answer to your "why" is much deeper than that. It goes back to knowing your purpose.

Here are a few questions to consider in figuring out your why. Take time to answer them before moving on.

- What makes you unique?

- What have you always been admired for?

- What words are often used to describe you?

- What comes easily to you that may be challenging for others?

- What difference do you make to your customers?

- What is that thing you do that only you can do?

- What is the reason you were born? (Okay, this one might take a little longer but it's well worth pondering!).

Why Do You Stay?

Knowing your why is important so that you can share it with your customers. I believe knowing why you stay is a pivotal point in your business. It will allow you to set new terms of engagement for you and your customers.

Thousands of advisors have left the industry and no one could blame them. Some have packed it in altogether; others will be back.

You've stayed, but you've set a new expectation for yourself. I've spoken to many advisors in the past two years who have said the same thing:

"I want to come back, but I want it to be different than before."

Your 10X travel business starts with you knowing your purpose and setting a new mission for yourself to come back bigger, better, and bolder than before.

Before you read any further, take out a piece of paper and complete these exercises.

1. Think back to your life's journey. What highlights and lowlights stand out for you?

2. What happened in your past, what did you make it mean, and how does it help you or hold you back?

3. What led up to the point where you joined the travel industry?

4. Why did you join?

5. What patterns do you see?

6. Why do you stay?

What do you want to do differently in the future?

Purpose is a lifelong commitment to becoming the best version of yourself.

If you only take away one concept from this book, let it be that fulfilling your purpose is noble, important, and lifegiving to you and everyone around you.

2. People
People are the plan.

Exponentially growing your business comes down to doing business you love with people you love.

Know your people.

If you invest in getting ten times better at knowing, finding, attracting, converting, servicing, and keeping customers, you don't need any other plan. People *are* the plan. Not just any people but *your* people.

Everything else you do becomes about how you do the people plan better.

It's like a good dinner party. If you have the right guest list, a set table, a good menu, and high heels, nothing can go wrong. If you have the wrong guest list, nothing else will make it right.

The very first step is to decide who your people are.

Your people are those who light you up, and who need what you are offering.

Who you serve is the most important shift of all because it allows you to stop being all things to all people. Rather, the goal is to become indispensable to a small group of raving fans.

Webster's definition of indispensable:

> *"So good or so important that you cannot manage without it."*

Think about it. Who in your client database would not leave home without running it by you? If you say no one, or very few, congratulations! People are your plan.

If you said most wouldn't, you'd still be doing well.

However, the data would say otherwise. Research shows that less than 30 per cent of customers return to the same travel agent.

Most agents are in a state of flux; so much has changed about knowing your people.

With Covid, the people whom you could reliably count on to travel are no longer keen to venture out. The people you least expected to hear from are ready to go tomorrow.

One agent explained how she learned never to assume she knew a person's propensity to travel.

Her long-time client had just undergone an extensive round of chemotherapy. She hesitated to reach out to her client, ruling them out of travel completely due to their medical situation. To her surprise, the client called and booked a month-long trip to Europe. They said they couldn't wait to travel — cancer be damned!

It's more important than ever to be visible and extend your offering beyond those you know, and what you think you know about them.

You need to be like a detective to find your people among the new travelers.

3. Process
Getting Things Done.

When asked how he became the GOAT (greatest of all time) basketball players, Michael Jordan replied:

"Step by step, I can't think of any other way!"
~ Michael Jordan

What Is a Process?

A process is a step-by-step method of creating a desired result.

A good process has a starting point and a series of recurring actions, it eliminates repetition or looping back, and helps us do more work in less time.

A key turning point for your business is understanding how to create a process that saves you time in *every* area of your business.

If you can find a way to produce a result in less time, you simplify your life.

Why Process Matters

The crossroad every travel advisor faces is that as you grow your travel business, you reach the maximum capacity in your ability to process the business.

Long before you reach your maximum earning potential, you run out of hours. You reach burnout and exhaustion.

The key is to create a process around revenue generating activities.

I once asked Michael Drever how he could dream and not get bogged down with all the work. He said it's simple.

I start every day with a simple t-chart on a piece of paper. On one side I write, 'Makes Me Money', on the other side I write, 'Everything Else'!

The goal is to go from overwhelmed to organized to elevated by implementing a process for doing the work that generates the greatest return on your time.

Here's what that journey looks like.

The Process Journey

① State: Overwhelmed

You looked up, and wondered where 2021 went. When you are overwhelmed, the business runs you. You are jumping from task to task, and it's exhausting.

You start each day with the intention of working on changing things, and then suddenly the day is gone and you don't know where it went. You are stuck and losing the will to keep going.

This is called being in the wall. It can last for days, weeks, months, and even years.

How I Feel: Exhausted

What I'm Doing: Quitting or taking a serious time out!

② State: Reactive

You are all over the map. You are literally putting out fires all day long, or jumping from task to task, doing something this way this time, and another way another time Doing it in the morning one day, and in the afternoon the next, instead of setting up the best time of day to do the same types of work.

The pandemic was a two-year-long reactive bonfire. As we pull out of it, we need to learn how to not jump from task to task.

How I Feel: Extreme

What I'm doing: Jumping around all over the place

(3) State: Replicate

You are seeing the value and investing in documenting tasks so that you can "do it once and use it often".

Recognizing patterns and finding ways to eliminate replicating your work is a significant way to turn the corner on productivity.

How I feel: Relieved

What I'm Doing: doing it once, using it often.

(4) State: Organized

You have created order in your work by grouping or batching like tasks together. Order includes organizing your tasks and creating key systems for managing the biggest parts of your role. It also includes executing tasks in the right order.

I discovered the importance of order when suddenly I had choices about when to do certain things during my day.

How I feel: Energized

What I'm doing: First things first, in 90-minute zones.

State: Elevated

The pinnacle of a good process is when your business can run without you. Far from robotic, it still needs you to do things that a machine cannot. However, everything that can be automated, systemized, documented, or reduced is in play.

How I feel: I feel exhilarated because it gives me room to do more of what I love.

What I'm doing: I'm working on my business, not in my business. I'm able to see my own system in my work.

In the next chapter, we will identify 10X strategies that allow you to create order and increase productivity with a systems approach to your business.

4. Performance
Better before bigger.

I'll never forget watching Joannie Rochette. She was the Canadian Olympic figure skater who lost her mother just two days before she was due to compete. She was visibly shaking with grief one minute and stepping onto the ice in front of the entire world the next. She made history.

What was unique about Joannie was her ability to channel her emotional energy into her performance. She skated for her mom and moved the entire world with her.

Thankfully, we're not called up often to perform under such extreme pressure. However, working these past two years has created a highly charged emotional landscape over a long period of time.

In order to create a 10X performance mindset, it cannot be about working harder.

You have endured so much.

It's about working better. Better always comes before bigger.

It's not just about getting better in general. It's about getting better at the things that light you up!

My son teaches guitar and always starts by asking, "What song makes you really happy every time you hear it?". He figures out how to get his students playing it within the first few lessons.

What's unique about 10X performance is that it encompasses more than just a number. A 10X performance metric includes setting goals for your own happiness. It's about full spectrum goal setting that includes getting everything you want out of life.

Instead of what gets measured gets done, consider these questions:

- What brings me the most joy?

- What do I love selling?

- What do I need to get better at?

- Whom do I love working with?

- Who will be with me when I am celebrating my wins?

For example, a simple goal might be to earn six figures, in half the time.

A full spectrum goal is to earn six figures so that you can travel with your family, build a dream home, take off six weeks a year, work four days a week, and give generously to people in need.

10X performance means setting goals for getting everything you want.

What if you don't know what you want? That is one of the most common challenges that derails goal achievement.

Recently, I was coaching a travel agency owner who was at the end of her rope. She was overwhelmed, exhausted, and ready to quit.

We tried setting a new goal for the business and it wasn't going anywhere.

When we dug in further she realized, she didn't know what she wanted! Prior to the pandemic, it was easy to think she wanted a thriving travel business. Now she wasn't so sure.

When we pressed in to what she wanted now, she suddenly teared up. *"I DON'T KNOW! I don't think I've ever really known. I have this business that I should love, and a great family. But I don't know what I want. I'm all over the place. The pandemic has kicked me down and I don't know if I want to get back up."*

I decided to take a different approach. Let's think about all the trimmings of a life well lived.

- What kind of relationships are important to you?

- Who do you love being when you are your best self?

- What brings you joy?

- What would you do with ten times more money if you had it?

- Who would you be celebrating with?

- Where would you travel to?

- What would you splurge on once a week if money were no object?

Sometimes, when you reverse engineer the process and — as Stephen Covey says — "Begin with the end in mind", suddenly you can visualize the dream-life.

You can only create a Mozart-worthy masterpiece that is worth putting in the 10,000 hours if you can visualize the concert.

If you can't picture the dream, complete with the people you care about at your side, no amount of coaching or hard work will get you there.

10X performance goals focus on the complete picture of success. Goals don't create happiness, they make happiness the priority.

Chapter Summary
The 10X Framework

- The 10X framework creates the foundation for getting ten times better in half the time.

- Your 10X travel business starts with you knowing your purpose and setting a new mission for yourself to come back bigger, better, and bolder than before.

- Who you serve is the most important shift of all because it allows you to stop being all things to all people. The goal is to become indispensable to a small group of raving fans.

- A process reduces the number of steps to create a customer. It eliminates repetition and helps us do more work in less time.

- 10X performance goals focus on creating happiness first and measuring it to improve it, rather than setting goals you are not attached to, then trying to figure out what to do.

Points to Ponder

- What is your why? Why did you start your travel business in the first place?

- How many of those reasons still exist today?

- What has happened during the pandemic that will help you be even more successful in the future?

- Whom do you love to serve? Identify your people.

- What do you notice about the patterns of your work? Do they feel random or organized?

- What could you do differently to create a more ordered approach to your day?

Part Three

The Four 10X Strategies

The purpose of the 10X approach to your business is to focus on strategies that will do two things: accelerate growth in your business and improve the speed at which you create customers.

The following four strategies allow you to grow at an exponential rate. But be careful: within each of these strategies lies an offsetting opportunity to do less.

The only way you can achieve everything you want without getting stuck in the details is to focus on growth and productivity at the same time.

The first is a strategy of connection. It involves having a clear intention to strengthen the value of your business through connection. Connection is like a muscle, it strengthens with use. It also weakens to the point where it can become damaging to your business if it is left unchecked.

Next, conversion. Every single prospect is an opportunity to grow your business. This strategy focuses on increasing your ability to turn suspects into prospects, prospects into friends, and friends into customers.

The third strategy is to be commercial. This refers to the way you earn more money in less time. Every customer experience you enhance is an opportunity to increase your revenue.

The final strategy is impact. You could say that this is the first strategy. This is about fulfilling your purpose. This strategy puts your vision and all the trimmings as the primary motivator for what you do. This allows you to make a difference so that, ultimately, all the hard work is worth it to you.

Without your desire to make an impact, it is easy to lose interest in your business. It is your True North.

Let's review each of these strategies in detail.

Chapter 4

10X Connection: Connection Is Currency

The connection you have with your prospects and past customers is the only true measure of the value of your business.

You may know thousands of people, but unless you are connecting with them for the purpose of creating customers, they are not an asset to your business.

If your business was a romantic relationship, you would be in the friend zone!

I consider my husband, Cam, to be the world's greatest salesperson. He once had a very long-time prospect, whom he had been courting for years, say to him, *"Cam, you are the nicest person I have never bought from"*.

Ugh, the friend zone can be painful!

The goal is to deepen the level of connection you have with your prospects to the point where you have a predictable source of income.

The connection you have with your list is worth more than money in the bank. Digital transformation experts, CSG Solutions ask:

> *"What is your business's greatest asset?*
> *Many would say money in the bank, but in reality,*
> *this particular asset is simply an effect;*
> *its cause is far more valuable. Money comes*
> *from your customers, and understanding these*
> *customers is key to creating more value within*
> *the business."*

The Size of Your List

How many people do you need on your list in order to generate a steady flow of high-income leads?

The answer depends on your level of connection with that list.

Consider the biggest and smallest weddings you've ever attended.

The size of a wedding says a great deal about connections. There's no question that a wedding with 1500 people says something different about the bride and groom than a wedding of 10.

They might be deeply networked in their community, or they might come from a culture of big weddings. It could be the bride's third wedding. Each says something different about the guest list.

What does your database say about you?

You are the epicentre of your database. Your relationship with the contacts speaks volumes about how connected you are to your business.

I met a travel agency owner who was a marketing wiz. He jumped in early to the trend of purchasing key domain names. He was able to secure several wedding sites for major sun destinations including Aruba, Jamaica, and others. Five years later, he realized he had no interest in being in the wedding planning business.

He had a massive database that required him to build out a business plan to support it. He had become trapped by his own success. He detested working with brides and wedding planners.

The size of the database is not nearly as important as your relationship to the human beings on your list.

Another agency owner works at the other end of the spectrum. Jenny has 450 people in her database. She knows every single person on her list. She has booked most of them multiple times. Her small, highly qualified list generates 4.5 million in sales.

She focuses on high-end bucket-list trips such as Africa, India, and world cruises.

More importantly, she travels with a small group of her people twice a year to somewhere exotic.

Her new post-pandemic 10X goal is to bring her daughter into the business. She is not giving her any of her leads. She is teaching her how to find, cultivate, and close her own list of people so that she can engage lifetime relationships.

The sweetest part of this story is that Jenny's mother taught her the business in the same way thirty years ago.

Jenny is teaching her daughter to be a master craftswoman. She is teaching her the art of curating lifetime relationships that become lifetime travel customers.

The key takeaway is that the size of the list is not as important as the quality of your connection with it.

The Importance of Connection

Connection is about keeping the flame alive in your relationships with every person on your list. It can be a slow burning ember, or from time to time a bonfire.

The key is to keep the connection so that when the time is right, your connection leads them to you.

Here are four enduring principles of connection.

 Connection is the meaning behind why you do this business.
Connection is the reason for your journey. You're not here to sell widgets or even travel. You're here to make vacation dreams come true. You simply cannot sell anything well without some kind of connection to the purpose of the trip.

The warmer that connection, the more meaningful the relationship, the more transformational the experience is for both you and your customer.

Advisors who continued to reach out to their contacts, even through pandemic-times, were rewarded with overwhelmingly positive feedback.

One advisor shared with me, "The most challenging part about calling isn't picking up the phone, it's getting the person off the phone. It feels incredible to make someone's day talking about travel!".

Connection is a leading indicator of future business.
Connection can only truly be measured when it converts to a sale. However, you can improve your odds of converting contacts into customers by acting on other leading indicators of engagement such as reading newsletters, attending events, and having warm conversations.

When someone goes into your website, it's like they are in your virtual store — a leading indicator that they are shopping to buy something. Perhaps not today, but travel is on their mind.

A shop keeper wouldn't dream of letting someone out the door without asking how they can help. Yet so often we see traffic on our website and we don't dig deeper to find out how we can help.

You can use strategies such as lead magnets and enticing calls to action to help raise the visibility of the connection.

 Connection makes calling easier!
I publish a newsletter every two weeks.

I also call my contacts every week. Sometimes I call 15 people, other weeks I call 5. The easiest calls to make are to the people who avidly read my newsletter.

If someone is opening every newsletter you send, or liking your posts on Instagram, pick up the phone!

They are highly engaged and you have something to talk about!

What did you like about my newsletter or post? Is there anything else you'd like to see me share?

Warming up your list with marketing nudges puts an end to cold calling.

 You are only as good as your last connection. Contacts cool quickly and eventually die. Research shows it takes eight touch points on average to convert to a sale. Yet we often go months and in some cases years between meaningful connections.

When you look at your database, ask yourself what percentage of these prospects are most likely to travel in the next 12 to 24 months.

Often, a database becomes cold because we never want to admit that someone is no longer a high-value connection. People move away, our focus on what we sell shifts, or in the case of Covid, some of our best connections are sitting out until things get "back to normal".

Or maybe, just maybe, the customer has booked elsewhere. Travel advisor Amy Donald shared with me,

"Here I was thinking they wouldn't want to travel, and I find out they booked a 14-day South Pacific cruise directly with the cruise line! I learned the hard way not to assume I know what my clients are thinking about Covid and travel."

The longer you leave it between connections, the harder it gets to make contact.

Reach out and take the temperature.

That means connecting with your database without trying to sell anything.

The simple truth is that connections either grow or die. There are so many ways to keep the flame alive.

Create a System to Capture and Nurture High-Value Customers

Your database is the single most lucrative 10X asset you have. It is the gateway to massive growth and improved productivity.

The goal is to create a database like Jenny's; a small, intimate collection of like-minded travelers who have a high propensity for future travel.

To achieve the optimal list, you need a system to constantly grow, nurture, and release contacts. People age out or move on so it is never a stagnant list.

Two years is a long time in the life of a senior. Sadly, some may have moved past their prime travel years. Others have moved into the empty-nester phase and are ready to make up for lost time and make the most of being kid-free!

Ultimately, you want the greatest number of bookings from the smallest number of travelers. The more you know your connections, the better you can deliver outstanding experiences.

You may be starting with a very small list that you need to grow. Or you may have a massive list and limited connection to those on it. If you cannot recall a single significant thing about your contacts, it's time to either deepen your relationship, or release them.

The first step is to identify the type of contact that you want to have on your list.

Connections come in three categories.

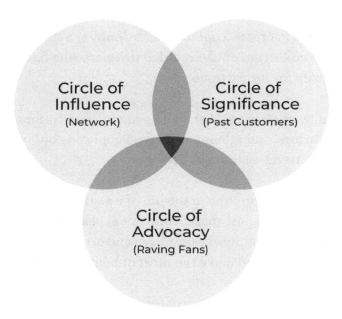

- **Circle of Influence** (Network):
  Those who are not yet captured on your list though you do have influence over them. They are your target market. You must be able to find and reach them in some way.

- **Circle of Significance (Past Customers):**
  Those who are significant to you. They are your past customers. You know they will book again, when the time is right.

- **Circle of Advocacy (Raving Fans):**
  They are ideal customers. They buy from you and they bring others to you.

Here is a breakdown of each segment, and how you can capture each connection as currency by creating a system that improves over time.

Circle of Influence (Network)

A circle of influence is a segment of your community that you've identified as your target market.

You have identified them as potential customers but they are not yet in a committed relationship with you.

Your circle of influence is somewhere within the following five stages. Let's review each stage, as well as the actions that would move them up the ladder.

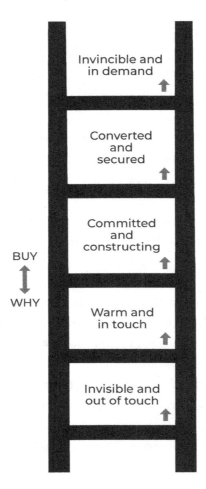

Invisible and Out of Touch

You know them but they have no idea who you are!

In this stage, you've identified your target market. You know who they are, what their travel motivations are, where to find them, and how to reach them.

Yet you are not known to your target market. You have not revealed yourself to them.

You are hiding or not sharing your genius with them!

Action Required:

Get visible!

> *"Visibility creates opportunity!"*
> ~ ***Koka Sexton, Social Media Guru***

It's time to come out from behind the curtain and be visible.

In this stage, you want to do all you can to ensure that the right customers are in your path.

- Social media is the perfect vehicle to become known to your target market.

- Networking is another ideal way to grow your influence within a target market. Where do your ideal customers hang out? Go there and be among them.

- Influence by association. Are there high-profile people within your network who might know the types of people you want to attract? LinkedIn first and second connections are ideal for this.

- Social-media influencers.

- Common pages that you and your target market like and follow.

The key to becoming visible to your target audience is to share content generously that builds interest and awareness. The goal is to build knowledge and trust over time.

Warm and In Touch

In this stage, prospects are known to you *and* they know you.

You begin the long game of warming them up! This is rarely an overnight win — unless the timing is perfect and they are ready to buy.

In this stage, you are doing all of the right marketing actions so that when the time is right, you're the first person a potential client thinks of. Even then, leaving this to chance is risky, as they are likely in this stage to consider more than one person who can do what you do.

Action required:

Get them on the phone!

At this stage, no matter what action you take to warm them up, it almost always leads to a phone call. You have their email address and phone number. You have permission to be in a committed relationship with them. This is an amazing milestone.

Warming up your prospects makes calling so much easier!

Committed and Curious

This is a very exciting stage because you've raised the awareness to the point of action. The prospect is ready to buy.

Wait, you are not confirmed yet until you both agree to be moving forward. Be careful of the curious prospect who may be shopping you.

Action required:

At this stage, you need to ask for the business and prepare the quote. This is the discovery phase, and its primary action is to ask thoughtful questions and to listen with interest.

Converted and Secured

Ask for the business and secure the sale! This is the much anticipated and highly celebrated stage. You've asked all the right questions, prepared, and presented the best of all options. Your prospect says yes!

They are no longer a prospect. They are now a customer!

Action required:

The best thing you can do to secure that customer is to add experiences to the booking.

Flights, hotels, insurance, excursions, special occasion items. All the extras "stick the booking" and make it much harder to cancel.

Invincible and In Demand

You've come a long way from invisible to invincible!

When you do this right, all those warm touches, generous tips and insights, invitations and stories, all lead to a celebration of the progress you've made!

To your customer, you are invincible. They wouldn't think of leaving home without you!

When you deliver the wow, it puts you in demand.

Action required:

Ask for a referral! A happy customer is likely to bring their friends who are just like them to your business.

Give yourself a big pat on the back! You are ready to move this client up from the circle of influence to the circle of significance.

Circle of Significance (Past Customers)

Your circle of significance are your satisfied past customers.

This section is dedicated to customer retention. Early in my travel career, I heard a meme that always stood out for me.

"They will book again; make sure they book with you!"

Sadly, according to companies such as Holland America and Royal Caribbean, less than 40% book with the same travel agent twice.

Not because they were unsatisfied. According to Vicki Freed, Senior Vice President of sales, people book elsewhere because their advisor was indifferent.

In other words, the client didn't know how much you care about getting them to book again.

Sometimes, you intentionally "let clients go". You are not meant to work with everyone.

However, it's often a matter of life getting too busy that time slips by and you haven't followed up. As a result, "clients cheat on you" says Freed.

When you pour so much of what you do into every transaction, it's disheartening when clients leave.

The goal is to be sure you keep one hundred percent of the clients you love. Clients who wholeheartedly support your values.

As Simon Sinek states:

> "The goal is not to sell to everyone who needs what you have.
> The goal is to find people who believe what you believe. "

There are three important steps to nurturing your Circle of Significance

 Never let a valued past customer get more than 30 days away from you.
From welcome home to meaningful touchpoints in between, past customers need to be nurtured.

Set a cadence of regular communication including newsletters, social media engagement, phone calls and events.

 Set a next call date every time you speak.
One of the easiest ways to keep in touch is put a 'next call date' in your calendar. You simply set it and forget it!

Choose a date that makes sense to your customer such as by when they plan to travel again and milestones.

 Ask. Never take rebooking for granted. A happy customer will tell ten friends. An unhappy customer might tell 100 or more.
Here are a few questions to help ensure customer retention.

- Can I get your next trip underway?

- When are we doing this again?

- How can I start your travel dreaming?

Circle of Advocacy (Raving Fans)

A circle of advocacy is a small but very powerful and lucrative segment of your business. They are your ideal customers, also known as your raving fans.

This segment travels solely based on your sage wisdom and recommendations. Advocates simply would not leave home without consulting with you.

They rave almost as much about working with you as they do about the travel itself.

You are so good, not only can they not ignore you, they will shout your name from the rooftops.

The key to leveraging the circle of advocacy is to be very clear about who is in it, and ensuring that they know they are in it!

Step one is to invite people from your circle of significance to become advocates.

When you first identify your ideal past customers, it's tempting to put everyone into your circle of advocacy.

However, there are ideal customers, and then there are advocates. The deciding factor *is do they or will they recommend you?*

The only way to identify and grow this list is to start asking every past customer for a referral or recommendation.

If you are hesitant to ask for a referral, they are not advocates for your own reasons; you're not sure and are afraid to ask.

Make it easy on yourself and create a process for asking *every* past customer for a referral.

Not only will you create the compounding impact of building an entire business based on referrals, but you will also identify your advocates for future marketing campaigns.

When you don't ask, you run the risk of a dissatisfied customer sharing a bad experience. We all deliver subpar service from time to time.

You are not perfect. Knowing the answer to the question "Will you recommend me?" can create a customer service save. At the very least, you mitigate the risk of a dissatisfied customer spreading a bad word.

Step two is to ensure your advocates know the benefits of being part of your inner circle.

This can be small gestures such as phone calls, updating their profiles, or sharing recent travel news that they would personally benefit from knowing about.

Benefits should also include some larger privileges such as early invitations to events, special departures or promotions.

Your advocates may also enjoy a seat at your table. Consider creating your own advisory board, inviting your very best customers to weigh in on important decisions you're making about your travel business.

When you're ready, an escorted advocates cruise is the perfect way to maximize the experience for you and your best customers.

Key Takeaway: Connection

The key takeaway to capturing and nurturing high-value customers is that it is like investing in your own happiness.

You are creating a database full of people you love working with.

When you do work you love with people you love, you never work a day in your life! That is quintessential 10X thinking!

Chapter Summary
10X Connection: Connection Is Currency

- The connection you have with your prospects and past customers is the only true measure of the value of your business.

- The size of the database is not as important as the quality of your connection with it.

- The four principles of connection: connection is the meaning behind the business; connection is a leading indicator of future business; connection makes calling easier; and you are only as good as your last connection.

- To achieve the optimal list, you need a system to constantly grow, nurture, and release contacts.

- A circle of influence is a segment of your community that you've identified as your target market, but they have not yet purchased from you.

- There are five stages involved in moving from influence to significance. Take action in each stage to move from invisible to invincible. The key is to get visible and in their path!

- Your circle of significance is made up of your past customers who believe what you believe and value what you value. The goal is to have a relationship that is so deep that every sale is a win-win!

- Your circle of advocacy is made of your raving fans! They would not think of traveling without you and they will shout your name from the roof tops:

  - Step one is to invite people from your circle of significance to become advocates.

  - Step two is to ensure your advocates know the benefits of being part of your inner circle.

Points to Ponder

- How strong is your connection with your database?

- How could you improve your overall connection with your circle of influence?

- What are your best practices for connecting with people to warm them up?

- When calling prospects, where do you start?

- What are your best practices around connecting with your circle of significance?

- What is the one thing you could do to increase business with your circle of significance.

- What is your current practice when asking for referrals?

- How would asking a client from your circle of significance for a referral improve your connection with them?

- How would inviting everyone in your circle of significance for a referral in order to become part of your inner circle benefit them? How would it benefit you?

Chapter 5

10X Conversion:
The Art of Creating High Value Customers

"Do what you do so well that they will want to see it again and bring their friends too."

*~ **Walt Disney***

When you attract ideal customers and provide indispensable service, they come back. They tell their friends and their friends' friends to come too. Et voila, you have a database of raving fans!

If only it was that easy.

Yes, delivering the outstanding service that creates a customer and a referral is at the heart of conversion, but every single client is different.

Getting the referral is only the first step. You must equally impress the new customer.

Working with referrals also increases the risk. You now have not one, but two customers at stake.

Nothing is more frustrating than referring a friend to a service provider that doesn't deliver for them.

We had a contractor who turned a small kitchen project into a renovation nightmare. He simply overcommitted himself and took months to finish a project that should have taken weeks. The quality of the work was so inferior that we scrapped it altogether and hired a new contractor to start again.

The referral came from a family member. The contractor was her brother-in-law. We didn't say anything about it so as not to ruffle the family feathers. Yet, had this been another customer of his, we would have shared our experience and he would have lost both of us.

A raving-fan strategy makes sense. It's simple to understand, and it can grow your business in all the best ways! However, without attention to the details like upping your customer service delivery, it can all fall apart for you.

The objective of a 10X conversion strategy is to have an efficient way to attract and retain customers. You also need to be intentional in skilling up to become the best in the world at what you do. This will greatly reduce your marketing costs when people begin to come to you.

Let's explore each of these as we unpack our second strategy: conversion.

Conversion: creating a steady stream of high-value customers through attraction, retention, and skilling up.

Customer Attraction

Filling up Your Pipeline with Ideal Prospects

In order to create a steady stream of high-value clients, you must begin with the idea that every customer will be a customer for life from the very first sale. In fact, it starts from the moment you make yourself visible to them.

In his best-selling book, *Customer for Life,* Carl Sewell suggests not viewing a customer as a single transaction, but considering them a customer for life from the moment they pull into the parking lot.

A Safeway customer isn't worth the $3.50 profit from a single sale; they are worth a family of four buying groceries twice a week for 25 years. That customer is worth over $750,000.

In the same way, the benefit of serving travel customers over a lifetime of trips is profound and circular. They buy more, you know them better, and they eventually buy more upscale experiences.

Recognizing the significance of the very first sale changes everything about how you optimize customer attraction.

What Is Customer Attraction?

The first step is to understand what customer attraction is.

Customer attraction is the sum of the activities that put you in the path of your ideal customer. It includes marketing, social media, your website, your online presence, newsletters, warm touchpoints, and — most importantly — calling.

Customer attraction is the signal you send to the market that you are open for business for these types of clients.

The thing that sets you apart from your competition is the way you deliver the travel experience during every step of the customer journey before, during, and after the trip. YOU are the experience that people like this need.

- **Customer attraction is** the art of starting the journey with lifetime customers.

  If you want to build a business working with people you enjoy, you need to make the first move. This is where many advisors get stuck. Whether it's the fear of rejection or the fear of the unknown, picking up the phone is hard.

Luckily, cold calling is unnecessary! There are many ways to warm people up before calling them.

- **Customer attraction** is the sum total of everything you do to warm up the phone call. It is creating informative content that drives website visitors, sharing newsworthy newsletters, posting engaging content on social media that adds value to your target audience.

- **Customer attraction means staying in contact.** There's a saying that I love which is, "Never let a good customer get more than 30 days away from you."

  Whether it's someone new you're courting or a past client, you are always keeping the flame alive.

- **Customer attraction is** being attractive. Your audience cares about what you're doing on their behalf. Improving your skills, becoming better, and serving clients just like them are all interesting and important ventures.

  Your message about what you care about is all part of the customer attraction process. Your why, and why it matters to you, is something people can really rally behind.

The Key to Customer Attraction

The key to well-executed customer attraction is to make it easy to execute and to never miss — ever.

Simplicity and consistency are the keys to your 10X success.

In fact, becoming ten times better at executing a fast and effective customer attraction program will give you the biggest results in the shortest amount of time.

The trap most travel entrepreneurs fall into is one of two extremes. They get so caught up in all things social media that they lose sight of its purpose. At every conference, advisors flock to hear the social media experts extoll the benefits of social media.

The experts are not wrong. It is a remarkable medium. However, at times they miss the fact that an advisor has to be an advisor first. You may not need every tool in the kit.

Unfortunately, far too often when I speak to advisors after they've taken a social media course, they become overwhelmed, lose intertest, or they bow out altogether.

In addition, one of the occupational hazards of growing your social media presence is the endless scrolling that can lead to deep levels of depression and despair.

The solution lies in putting social media into perspective of what you are trying to achieve. Connection!

The goal is to increase visibility in order to deepen relationships with your ideal clients.

Here, we will examine those in more detail.

Your Marketing System

Marketing plays a critical role in warming up and engaging all three circles within your database.

Once you decide on whom you are targeting, the goal is to create an effective way to reach them consistently and frequently in the least amount of time.

The diagram below shows the components of a simple marketing system that integrates your marketing.

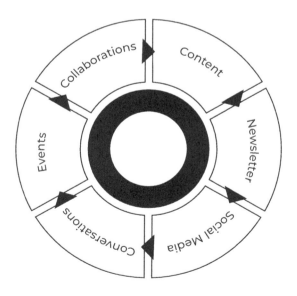

Content

Your content is the message you want to put out into the world that sets you apart. It is the signal to your ideal customer that you have a solution to their problems. You're passionate about inspiring them to travel and to book with you.

Everyone can post the latest celebrity ship, or how fabulous it is to take a river cruise. Why should your target audience care about hearing it from you?

That content needs to live somewhere (such as a content repository) so it's easy to access internally.

The 10X approach to content creation is, "Create it once, use it often".

The ideal content plan includes:

- Tips on travel

- News and notes

- Customer experience and testimonials

- Destination focus of the week

- Travel inspiration

- Something about you which creates trust.

Create your content once per month in advance, leaving a few holes for breaking news.

Always include your advice (why this?), your positioning (why you?), and urgency (why now?).

Newsletters

A newsletter is the most effective way to reach your target market consistently. It's a weekly or bi-weekly message that provides tips and insights on travel.

The mistake most agencies make is to create a newsletter that is price-driven. They spend untold hours cumulating information that changes before you can put the cat out.

A newsletter that builds a sense of belonging to your community is far more powerful. Your views on travel, best places to travel, new travel trends, best client trip, girlfriend getaway pics, etc., are all far more compelling than "Go to Mexico for $999".

You need to feature products, however, put everything in the context of *why:* why this, why you, why now?

People don't read, they skim. Your name popping in their inbox every other week is enough to keep you front of mind for when they want to open and peruse, or they are ready to buy.

Social Media

Social media creates visibility within your target market. It is an effective way to share your "why" with the world. You can effectively position travel your way, for people you care about. The simple, most impactful way to execute your social media plan is a combination of your content and your newsletter.

Create a content repository, then build a bi-weekly or weekly newsletter.

Then, strip out the best quotes, tips, deals, and news to create three to five separate posts each week.

Marketing services such as the programs provided by your host or consortia are fantastic ways to keep up visibility without you doing the work. They are a no brainer. In fact, you should evaluate your host based on the quality and consistency of their marketing programs.

However, to ensure you are adding your advice (why this?), positioning (why me?), and a sense of urgency (why now?), it's important to personalize your marketing message.

Conversations

One-on-one conversations are critical to communicating with your ideal customer. They are a two-way experience and vital to deepening the connection.

Vicki Freed, SVP of Sales for Royal Caribbean says, "Emails are a monologue, phone calls are a dialogue".

You can and must warm up your database with content, newsletters, and social media. However, the best way to move a client from prospect to buyer is to create the opportunity for a sales conversation.

I stress "opportunity" as not every phone call must result in a sale. Every phone call is about building trust so that when the client is ready, you're the first person they think of.

Events
Events are a closing tool. When a prospect is not ready to travel, much less book travel, events are a soft close to help clients keep an open mind. In these post-pandemic times, something magical happens when your best customers witness other customers committing to travel.

When people can see others jumping on the bandwagon, FOMO kicks in. People may be reluctant to book, yet nobody wants to be too late and miss out on an ideal booking window.

In the midst of uncertainty, events help your customers feel like they are not alone. An event can also rekindle a customer's desire to travel that may have become dormant after not thinking about it for so long.

Collaborations

An effective collaboration can create a win-win solution and attract more ideal customers.

Winemakers, sommeliers, chefs, dancers, choirs, chess players... the list of possible collaborations is endless. These are affiliations that have memberships or a following.

The collaborative must have influence over people you would consider ideal customers. Don't make the mistake of giving away the moon, only to find out that there is little-to-no opportunity to win clients as a result; open the doors for your services.

They must meet regularly or have a loyal following.

Collaborations create win-win opportunities to expand your circle of influence.

Ask your best customers what interests they have in common. Watch your social media feeds to find out who they are following.

You are like a detective looking for clues!

Partners

There are always people in your network who have as much to gain from your success or happiness as you do. Partnerships are relationships with investors, consortia, hosts, and highly interested friends and family and the like.

In the same way delighted customers rave about you and your service, partners are keen to help!

The key with partners in your business is to be easy to refer to. Create an "About Me" document that is easy to share.

Reach out to them on occasion to remind them of your "why" and who you serve.

For example, *I curate high-end vacations for empty nesters. If you know anyone celebrating a big milestone or who wants a deep level of expertise in Europe, please send them my way.*

You never know when someone is going to ask someone very close to you for help with a specific trip. However, because you are out of sight and not necessarily front of mind, the referral doesn't take place.

Customer Retention

The Service Wow Without Going Overboard.

The single most important customer retention strategy is delivering service that creates customers for life.

In the previous chapter, we reviewed the high-level actions for moving contacts from your circle of influence, to significance, then to your circle of advisory. The key action is to make sure customers will book again with YOU.

Customer retention is a deeper strategy of delivering the 'wow.' It's about becoming indispensable to a highly qualified database.

The service wow impacts the current vacation and every vacation you will sell in the future.

However, there is a limit to how much you do in the name of service.

In this chapter, our retention strategy will highlight areas in which you can do less to achieve more.

Service has two edges. Too little and you will lose customers. Too much and you may be doing more than the customer needs or wants. As a result, you put in too much time and are not paid your worth.

It is easy far too easy to go overboard. In this trap, you tend to do things for clients that they are not ready for or haven't asked you for.

For example, spending time researching hotel options, without the primary vacation confirmed.

Research of any kind can be exhausting, even when the main event is confirmed. The rabbit hole is so deep that before you know it, you've spent hours online and found ten options instead of three.

The only way to create a 10X customer retention strategy is to find the balance. You must become 10 times better at delivering customers the right level of service so that you can do it in half the time.

To achieve the balance, you need to be outstanding at the following three skills.

Better questions, bigger business

Asking better questions involves using better language that gets the customer to open up. Better questions also help you pay more attention to the answer.

Try to cue up twenty questions that you don't know the answers to, or that might surprise you with the response.

These questions are setting you up for flawlessly executing your recommendations.

They will save you so much time when it comes to the research phase. Better questions are like investments. The things you learn on an initial discovery call may save you hours of time and money in future marketing initiatives.

For example, the question "What are your top three bucket list destinations?" plants the seed and lays the groundwork for future travel.

Narrow Your Scope of Customers

As we've already learned, you cannot be all things to all people.

The more similar your customer segments are, the more familiar you will be with suitable options. Specialize in customers first. You will find that a pattern emerges in the types of products you recommend, thereby greatly reducing the amount of product knowledge you need to retain.

Narrow the Range of Products Presented

Creating a list of preferred suppliers is a 10X strategy. It narrows your scope and will earn you higher commissions and derive more support as you become more meaningful to those suppliers.

That is not to say ignore what the client has asked you for. Unless the product is a complete disaster and a risk to your clients, always present the product your clients asked for so the client feels heard.

However, include two other options. A similar, highly preferred option, and an elevated, luxury option.
At that point, you must be skilled at outlining your recommendation to the client so that it becomes an easy decision for them.

We'll cover more on the power of recommending in threes later in the next chapter.

It's important to note that your products reflect your brand and choosing them well can make a significant difference to your customer retention or customers-for-life strategy.

Chapter Summary
10X Conversion: The Art of Creating High Value Customers

- In order to create a steady stream of high-value clients, you must begin with the idea that every customer will be a customer for life, from the moment you are visible to them.

- The key to well-executed customer attraction is to make it easy to execute and to never miss — ever.

- Put social media into the perspective of what you are trying to achieve: connection!

- The purpose of social media is to increase visibility in order to deepen relationships with all three circles, but particularly with your circle of influence.

- Marketing plays a critical role in warming up and engaging all three circles within your database. Each of the following areas must be executed accordingly:

  - Content — Create once, used often, in all areas of marketing.

  - Newsletters — Send quality messages consistently to all three circles.

- Social Media — Create positioning and visibility to increase influence.

- Conversations — All attraction marketing culminates with a phone call.

- Events — A high-touch approach for connecting more broadly .

- Collaborations and Partnerships — Leverage your network to increase visibility with adjacent communities.

- The single most important customer-retention strategy is to deliver service that creates customers — for life.

- Service has two edges. Too little and you will lose customers. Too much and you are not paid your worth.

- There are three key ways of maximizing the return on your retention programs:

  - Better questions, bigger business

  - Narrow your scope of customers

  - Narrow the range of products presented.

Points to Ponder

- What does it take to create a customer for life in your business?

- What can your best customers teach you about how to attract new customers?

- What marketing activity do you do the most consistently?

- What marketing activity could you increase that would increase your sales the most?

- What is stopping you from executing it?

- How could you do a very simple version of it?

- How could asking better questions save you time?

- How could asking better questions grow your business?

- Who could you say no to in order to make room for more ideal customers?

- How could you reduce the number of products offered?

- What impact would it have on your business?

Chapter 6

10X Commerce: Earn More Money in Less Time

For as long as I can remember, the travel industry has justified lower pay in exchange for the marvellous fringe benefits of travel. Yet over the years, travel perks have become few and far between.

There are blackouts, limited inventory, and red tape. Suppliers often expect time, effort, and a return on their investment in your perk. This is understandable, yet sometimes defeats the point.

The occupational hazard of traveling with a client's best interests in mind is like sleeping with one eye open.

It's still sleep, but it's not as restful.

This is not to say that travel perks are not important. On the contrary, they are vital to your expertise.

Whether you're doing an intensive trip or a family vacation, traveling is an integral part of your ongoing education.

However, using it as full compensation is robbing yourself of some degree of value.

Positioning travel perks as purely incremental helps ensure you are getting paid the full value of your work.

In this chapter we will examine how to 10X your commercial strategy.

Your 10X Commercial Strategy
To increase revenue per transaction through selling, upselling, cross selling, and fees.

Commission and Compensation
The big-picture view of your compensation starts with your base commission. Commissions range from 8 to 18 per cent, depending on the travel supplier.

For the most part, the base commission is not nearly as variable as the other factors, such as sales volume, upselling revenues, and add-on sales.

Cruises, for example, hover around the 15 per cent mark.

The reason for this is that suppliers try to keep competitive and fair commission policies in place.

If you know that 80 per cent of your sales volume is coming from 20 per cent of your suppliers, your goal is to ensure you are earning top-tier commission with those partners. In turn, you want to ensure that for most clients you remain committed to offering those core partners.

It is also important to do the math and consider the commission combined with the average selling price. It may be that one of your core partners offers less commission, but they are your go-to partner based on all the other factors such as the onboard guest experience, range of itineraries, and superior customer service.

A slightly lower commission on a higher selling price can make a huge difference, for example:

$2500 x 0.15 x 100 customers = $37,500

$10,000 x 0.12 x 100 = $120,000

You could argue that it is much easier to find 100 customers at $2500 than 100 customers at $10,000. That may be true, or may not.

The reality is that the market place is crowded at the lower price point level with both online and offline agencies.

The higher the price, the greater the need for the advice of a knowledgeable travel advisor. The higher the price points, the fewer number of advisors who can sell it.

Selling at a higher price point may seem harder at face value, but less competition, more need for advice, and a much higher total compensation make a compelling argument for becoming highly skilled at it.

Tour Conductor Revenue
Tour conductors are one of the most lucrative financial incentives in the market. If there is a one-in-ten tour conductor ratio, you can earn thousands of dollars in additional commission.

What most agents don't consider is how much additional work is involved in curating a high-end group experience.

The tour-conductor revenue allows you to build in value for the group and compensate yourself for the additional effort.

A word of caution: be careful not to give it away. Tour conductors are part of your overall commercial strategy. They are also an important revenue source for adding extra touches for the group.

Decide in advance what incremental revenue a host may bring before you can offer them the tour conductor to travel.

Closing the Sale

The lion's share of your commercial strategy starts and ends with your ability to close the sale.

When you sell well, it's incredibly exciting for the customer. It's a sacred moment. That is why people call it the moment of truth. That moment when you've presented the best of all possible options. You've done your homework, you've listened well, and you've found something that has the potential to be a life-changing trip. It's not brain surgery, but it can create memories they will cherish forever.

Selling and presenting your recommendation well is like being the lawyer who says, "*Your honour, the defence rests its case*".

Most unsuccessful sales pitches can be attributed to disregard for this moment of truth. Here are a few of the most common mistakes.

 You give away free advice.
Your passion gets the best of you and you give away expertise without clarifying where the client is on their buying journey. If someone ghosts you after an hour or more of your time researching, or says it's not the right time right now, you've misread the moment.

2 You don't ask the right questions.
Much of what we are able to deliver in terms of an elevated customer service experience depends on the questions we ask. Better questions, bigger business. It's that simple.

3 You sell what you would recommend, rather than what the client's asking for.
You race to the product recommendation without listening to the client's needs. You are bombarded with promotions. You have preferred partners that you personally love to experience. Before you rush to judgment, keep asking questions until you know exactly what they are looking for.

4 You lose clients over Covid.
You can have the best recommendations and expert advice, yet you still lose them over Covid. The key is to be patient. Stay connected because when the time is right, you will be their first call.

The Solution to Closing the Sale:

1 Ask better, more thoughtful, trip-of-a-lifetime, questions.
Investing in a preplanned discovery conversation with a set agenda and a plethora of thought-provoking questions is one of the best ways to improve your chances of closing the sale.

There are no trick questions, misleading limited-time-only offers, or fake scarcity tactics that are going to work over the long haul.

Only a genuine interest in creating a lifetime customer through a deep and meaningful discovery process will yield the best result. A closed sale this time, and the groundwork for all future travel.

2 **Listen with interest and without judgement.**
It's easy to let your passion get in the way. Keep listening, stay calm, and take notes. Only interrupt or add to the conversation if you are recapping what you've heard.

Do not speak your mind. There will be plenty of time for that later. Your job is to get them over the bridge of indecision.

3 **Bring out their current state of knowledge, asking "What has your research told you so far?"**
Save yourself hours of aggravation by getting out on the table any half-truths or unfulfilled promises they have picked up during their own research.

4 **Bring on the Covid conversation, asking: "What is your knowledge of Covid and travel?"**
When you are selling, you are trying to offset a multitude of media messages, family member

misgivings, and government regulations swirling around the conversation at hand.

Stay calm and carry on.

 What is the MIP (most important reason) for the trip?
What is their vacation 'why'? Refer back to what matters most and clearly demonstrate how your travel recommendation fulfils their wish.

Service Fees
To fee or not to fee? Since the pandemic, there has been a sharp increase in the number of advisors who charge fees.

While fees vary depending on the scope of travel planning required, one thing is clear. **Advisors who charge fees earn more**; 40 per cent more, according to Host Agency Reviews.

One advisor, who calls himself The River Cruise King, claimed that he earned $20,000 in less than three months by charging fees.

There is no question that charging fees is lucrative. However, it also allows you to discern buyers from shoppers.

Over the past months, with extraordinary on-hold times with airlines and tour operators, travel advisors have become the most likely alternative for getting "free advice".

One client, Marie, was so exasperated with clients shopping her for free Covid and travel advice, she implemented a $99 "peace of mind" fee.

Her patter went something like this:

"I'd be delighted to give you all the travel information you need to ensure your trip with Air Canada that you are already booked onto is an enjoyable one; the 'peace of mind' fee is $99 and it includes the following:

- *Covid rules and regulations for up to three destinations*

- *Covid rules and regulations in Canada*

- *Covid testing information*

- *How and where to get your Covid test*

- *What to do if you get Covid in destination*

- *Covid and travel insurance*

- *A 15-minute travel consultation."*

While many people dropped out once they heard about the fee, to her surprise, she also had people take her up on the offer, either by switching their booking, or by paying the fee just for the advice, and generating a nice pipeline of leads for future travel.

According to Marie, it wasn't about the fee, it was about putting an end to the free advice!

Which leads to the important benefit of charging a fee. A fee puts an imaginary line between shopping and buying. One of my most highly regarded mentors says:

"Stay in the WHY before they BUY."
                                        ~ Matt Church

A conversation with a client is like the starting line at the NASCAR race. You are lined up and raring to sell travel! It's what you love to do! The client is also excited, and can't wait to start planning.

A fee is like raising the chequered flag and then pausing.

Before the flag drops, a fee allows you to create a compelling race plan. You can present a range of services you provide exclusively for your clients, and what this service will cost.

Charges range from $50 for a simple change fee, to $5,000 for planning a wedding. Most fall between $100 and $250.

One agency group met for weeks during the peak of the pandemic to determine what each charge should be. Creating the list together helped increase the buy in.

They also supported one another as they began to share the fees with clients. Rarely was there any push back.

Most clients somewhat expect the fees and have no issue paying them, according to sources I've interviewed.

Luxury travel advisor Ralph Lantosca introduced a flat rate planning fee of $5000 for 20 hours of travel consulting. He is now working with high-end customers, some of whom push 40 to 60 hours per year of consulting, and earning $250,000 in fees.

The challenge most advisors have is charging existing clients. This fear is soon put to rest when those existing clients cancel for the third time.

Charging fees is more than a revenue strategy. It is a time-saving technique that allows you to only invest in clients where closing the sale is inevitable.

Tapping Into the New Luxury Market

Luxury travel is the fastest growing segment of the travel industry. According to 'Luxury Travel Magazine', it's growing one third faster than every other segment. Luxury travel is expected to grow exponentially in the coming decade.

The opportunity to upsell lies in what is driving this growth. It comes from the following three key variables.

First is the demand for a new level of safety. In travel, safety translates to many things including privacy and space ratios. People want more space between themselves and other travelers.

According to the Amex Global Travel Trends Report, privacy is the new ultimate luxury: 75 per cent of respondents agreed that the experiences that offer ultimate privacy are becoming a key sought-after feature of luxury travel.

Second is the explosion of a new trend called 'masstige' — prestige for the masses. There is a general yearning for luxury touches in everything we do. Rather than two distinct classes, there is a blurred line between class and experience. Luxury lies in the experience itself, not in the price.

Consider the Covid test taken at a busy walk-in clinic versus the test taken in the comfort of your own home with an online doctor. One is a mass-market experience, the other is a luxury experience. Yet, the cost is higher for the mass market test than for the private test.

You get to choose based on your ability to figure things out, not based on price. That is pure masstige. A hidden luxury benefit available to all but only discovered by the clever elite.

Third is the sheer volume of potential travelers. For the first time in history, we have five generations of people traveling.

The Silent Generation (1926 to 1946): This group of senior travelers were robbed of their golden years of travel. They yearn to travel while their health allows it.

The Baby Boomers (1947 to 1961): This segment, the largest segment of travelers prior to the pandemic, are making up for lost time.

Gen X (1965 to 1980): They've been locked in Zoom rooms for two years and are ready for real-life experiences. Travel is a tonic for their weary souls.

Millennials (1981 to 1997): This is the first generation who were given an iPhone by the time they were 12. They have far greater expectations for an out-of-the-ordinary experience and, somehow, they are willing and able to pay for it. Perhaps it's because 56 per cent of this generation still live at home.

Gen Y: (1995 to 2007): Those in the technology generation have grown up figuring things out through apps. They demand a more diverse, inclusive and sustainable lifestyle, and they are taking those demands into the way they view travel.

The desire for transformational travel ahead of owning a home, car, or material possessions is qon the rise, especially with Generation Y. They would rather text than drive.

Matthew Upchurch, President of Virtuoso explained how his 23-year-old daughter has traveled the world but has never owned a car in her life.

While only 5 per cent of the workforce, GenY are driving their views through a fearless use of social media. They may have the greatest impact on all travel.

These five generations, though completely unique in their perspectives, share the common experience of the isolation of the Covid pandemic.

Traveling again offers an elevated opportunity to reconnect with humanity.

In the post-pandemic era, you have the opportunity to tap into the luxury trend through upselling and cross selling.

Let's review both as a core part of your commercial strategy.

Upselling

The art of upselling is to present options that increase your commission revenue.

The easiest way to do this is to present options they will buy at some point during their vacation. When they purchase those through you there is a benefit to them.

Another way is to present options that deliver a wow experience that costs more but is demonstrably worth it to the client.

As we learned in the sales chapter, sales is not based on tricks or slick techniques. There is no one-liner that is going to move someone from spending $5,000 to $10,000.

However, an integrated approach to positioning price and value can double or even triple the amount a client is willing to invest upfront in their vacation.

There are three ways to achieve this.

1. Fluency: upselling through comprehensive understanding of price and value.

2. Freedom to choose: upselling by comparing three options.

3. Fixed options: upselling through add-on components.

Upselling Through Fluency

Do the math! Ugh, I knew my dad was right.

When I was in high school, my guidance counsellor advised me that I did not need Math 12 in order to get into university.

Eureka! I could hardly wait to go home and tell my parents that Grade 12 just got a whole lot easier!

As you might have imagined, my father, a civil engineer by profession, was not having any of this nonsense.

"Math", he said, "Is what separates the winners from the losers". He also said, "It separates the men from the boys".

Coming from a family of three boys, I always loved being included in this frame. He didn't see me any differently than my brothers. He saw me as a force to be reckoned with, in a world that still showed a preference for male leaders.

Feeling humbled, but also knowing he was probably right, I went back to school to sign up for Math 12.

You don't have to be an engineer or a data scientist, but the key to winning in business is knowing your numbers.

Financial fluency means you understand how the revenue flows in your travel business. You are able to connect how the sales efforts you make impact the amount of money you earn.

The easiest and most effective way to upsell is to ensure as much of that spend as possible flows through you so that you can earn a commission on it.

If you can show that you are saving the client money by paying for it upfront, it is a win-win outcome.

There are two key competencies that have the greatest impact:

1 Providing ballparks and estimates.

2 Demonstrating the ROI.

Let's consider both of these mathematical talents.

Ballparks and Estimates

When I first learned how to sell cruises, I learned the power of "ballparks". Clients are looking for a general idea of how much their dream vacation will cost (e.g., $2500 for the cruise, about $1500 more to get into the suites and double for the top suite).

However, we take a giant risk when we quote a ballpark without knowing the kind of experience they are looking for.

I was hosting a river cruise event with high-end wine connoisseurs. One attendee glanced at the brochure, noticed a range of staterooms and asked, "What is the ballpark price for my wife and me to do this?".

Knowing the packages and inclusions, I quoted $10,000 to $20,000.

He looked back at me and said, *"How much would it be to do this right?"*... I was caught off-guard.

He wasn't looking for a price range, he was looking for an inclusion range. What out-of-the-box experiences could I offer him to meet or exceed his expectations? In the end he spent over $100,000.

I learned the value of knowing both the cost to upgrade to the top suite, as well as knowing the benefits included with that upgrade.

There is far greater demand for the most expensive suites than there is supply. This is not simply because there are more affluent people than you realize in your market. It's that the consumer always finds the deal, even if that deal costs $100,000.

As a product goes up in price, so does the value of intangible benefits that consumers are looking for.

For example, when a client knows they can host their entire family for cocktails every night before dinner, it puts a benefit before the cost.

It's not a private lounge area, it's a private lounge where you can enjoy a latte and catch up on some emails while the rest of the family is sleeping. The concierge will book all of your shore excursions, dining reservations and ensure you get on and off the ship ahead of the crowd.

Price Ranges — Understanding How Upper Limits Work
When you look online for a hotel, they have technology that enables you to put your price range into a scale. This allows a shopper to choose their upper and lower limit.

If you shop for a house, they also have ranges. Ranges are in $100,000 increments up to $2 million dollars. It then leaps up to $500,000 increments, and then eventually jumps by million-dollar brackets.

Human nature is that we want the hotel or the best house for the least amount of money.

When selling travel, giving people an upper limit range helps expand their expectations of what might be possible.

To be clear, you don't need to know these by heart. Nor do you need to blurt these without asking a full range of discovery questions.

However, being fluent in what a client might experience at the top of the range invites the client into the possibility mindset.

Then you must go to work on delivering the value.

If you're trying to get someone to buy up, you must be skilled at keeping people in the possibility mindset. It's much easier to remove items from their shopping cart than to add them back.

Demonstrate the ROI (Return on Investment)
People buy with their hearts and justify with their heads. Even if you're able to capture the hearts of your buyers (through the emotional journey you take them on), if you can't make the ROI case for working with you, you won't make the sale.

One of the most powerful tools in travel is to know the price and value of each travel purchase a la carte.

It is more expensive to add on all of the extras on a premium product than it is to do a luxury version of the same vacation.

Regent Seven Seas posts this price comparison on their website. This demonstrates the value of their all-inclusive pricing which helps consumers to justify the indulgence. At face value, the price of a luxury cruise compared to a premium cruise might be double.

When you add in all of the inclusions, they are nowhere near double. Yet the experience is extraordinary.

There is the convenience factor of not having to dip into their wallets every day.

The research shared by Regent is that their guests' satisfaction scores went through the roof once they started offering excursions. We all know life gets better when we truly live it!

Once guests have "paid" for the excursions in their all-inclusive price, they jump in with both feet! They have an amazing time and have something exciting to talk about at dinner.

Guests didn't have to think about the cost, or make to-buy-or-not-to-buy decisions throughout their cruise. The last thing we want to be doing on vacation is making value-based decisions.

After sitting at home for two years, people are eager to get out and explore if for no other reason than to have something interesting to talk about.

Painting a Picture of Value

Imagine you are on your private verandah as you sail into the shimmering Cancun harbour. Your butler brings you fresh blueberries and a cafe latte with two pumps of vanilla. He knows just how you like it because you ordered it that way on your first day.

He also confirms your dinner reservation at the ships private dining room and drops off your excursion tickets — you're taking a private flight to Chizinitzu — then, he leaves you to enjoy your morning view.

What value can you put on someone knowing how you love your coffee and delivering it to you? What would you pay to wake up to a spectacular morning at sea, or to share a wonderful exchange with a crew member who is going above and beyond to look after your every need?

You top that off with a private plane to see one of the Seven Wonders of the World. It's hard to imagine how many things had to take place for that moment to happen. What is it worth?

It's priceless.

The heart plays a much more significant role on influencing the head than most of us realize. Taking time to paint a picture for clients that helps them visualize how special these moments are is a crucial part of the sales process.

Freedom to Choose

I admit I used to be a 'House Hunters' junkie. Perhaps it's my secret life goal of being a home renovator or one of the savvy real-estate agents who made it look like such a worthwhile endeavour to help buyers find their "dream home".

In this show, they effectively demonstrated the rule of three. It goes as follows:

1. Always give clients what they asked for.

2. Give them something that is a slight stretch.

3. Give them something out of reach with an irresistible feature that feels like a dream home.

Here's how these rules play out in your business.

 Always give the clients what they asked for.

It's hard to present products that you don't believe in. While it's reasonable to have a setlist of approved suppliers, not presenting what they asked for can be very frustrating to the client.

It's far more powerful to present it along with your recommendation of its shortcomings based on what the client needs, not based on what you think.

When you say, *"Oh you don't really want that low-end property or cruise"*, or simply omit to present it, the client doesn't feel heard.

Instead, do the research, and say something like this:

"Here is the product you asked for. I recall you mentioned that safety was a primary concern. Unfortunately, this property doesn't offer any of the social distancing requirements that you were looking for."

 Always give the client something that is a slight stretch.

There are born five-star clients. The rest of us climb the luxury ladder one ring at a time. We dabble in upgrades to premium class, never to return to economy, especially on a long-haul flight.

We get the taste of a water view and then we understand the value of waking up to the dream landscape. We take endless photos, hoping to capture the lasting memory. When was the last time you took a photo of a courtyard view and said, "Never again"?

We experience the benefit of being greeted by a limo driver with a sign when the rest of the world is standing in a one-hour taxi line or facing an Uber shortage.

The feeling your clients get when they get the VIP treatment is the one they come back telling their friends about. Or they say to themselves, "Boy, does my travel agent know they're doing!".

Always provide luxury dabbles. Have an array of upgrade opportunities ready to present at every point in the customer journey.

 Always offer a luxury version of what they have asked for.

What would a fully expressed, luxury version of this experience look like?

The only way you can know whether something is truly out of the budget is to explore it with the client. The client doesn't always make the connection that the value of what's included in the price increases as the price goes up (we'll cover more about this in the next chapter on financial fluency).

Showing clients the fully loaded option will do one of two things. It will either inspire them that this is their time, or it may open their eyes to elements of the luxury version they can add to a more premium product.

Either way, you have elevated the experience.

Fixed Options — The Dabblers

We were wandering around the gift shop at the airport. My husband decided to check in on the flight to see if there were any changes to our departure time.

We'd rather arrive four hours early and relax than ever rush at the last minute. It had been so long since we'd gone through security, he felt it was time to check.

He returned 10 minutes later with a rather animated look on his face and this update: "They have oversold the economy section of the flight. They have two seats in premium economy available but they are charging $450 per seat!".

"I made a decision for us", he stated, seeming somewhat proud of himself.

I could not tell which way he went. Did I mention his Scottish heritage? Saving money was his go-to law for all decision making. Yet, he also knew this was a milestone trip for us as the first real vacation we'd had in years.

"What did you do?" I asked, almost accusing him of making the wrong decision.

Upgrading on an overseas flight for a fraction of the usual cost had only one answer (my offsetting "you only live once" approach to spending keeps us balanced).

I immediately cringed at my tone.

He showed me two new boarding passes: 3A and 3B.

"Eureka!"

We felt like we'd won the lottery!

This was the first of our many experiences dabbling in luxury.

We've added special touches to every trip we've taken since.

One time, I surprised him with a private gondola transfer in Venice. He was meeting me on a business trip and expected a two-hour transit via the local ferry system.

I arranged a private driver, combined with a spectacular Venetian water taxi to whisk us into the start of our Mediterranean cruise.

The cost of the transfer was $500 compared to the public transit cost of $80. The experience?

Priceless.

Dabbling in luxury is available to everyone. It's the masstige approach to upselling.

In order to execute luxury dabbling, you need to implement the combined learnings of upselling through fluency and the freedom to choose options.

First, through fluency.

As an advisor, your role is to be fluent in what a complete vacation experience from door to door includes.

For example, the main event, be it a cruise, tour, or independent land vacation. From there, you'll need to look after every component and offer a few that the client had not thought of.

The impact of both adding on each component and upgrading each element can be a gamechanger.

See how this breaks down.

Travel Option	Bare Bones	Premium Upgrades	Fully Loaded
Main event	$2,500	$2,500	$5,000
Transfer to airport		$80	$150
Pre-night airport hotel		$150	$300
Flight — with Mark Up		$1,500	$3,000
Pre package		$1,500	$3,000
Excursions x3		$300	$1,000
Post event		$1,500	$3,000
Insurance		$600	$875
Service fee		$200	$200
Subtotal	$2,500	$8,330	$11,750
	Bare Bones	Upgraded	Fully loaded
Commission earned	$375	$1,500	$2,300
x100 clients	$37,500	$150,000	$230,000

Why Upselling Matters

Effectively positioning the value of travel through fluency, the freedom to choose, and upgrading the fixed options is the key to becoming ten times more commercial.

However, the primary reason that upselling the sale matters is far more important than money.

The reason upselling matters most is that it increases the excitement to book and to remain booked.

After two years of on-again-off-again travel bookings, the best way to offset the pandemic is to make a complete shift in your approach to the meaning of travel.

It is about giving the trip its rightful place among life goals.

After two years of uncertainty, taking more time to ensure that travel is a priority is key.

Taking the time to position the sale as a life-changing experience for the client enables them to view the trip as something transformative; a life goal.

The world around us is changing. In addition to the pandemic, there's an evolution of awareness about our humanity.

Social justice and increased inclusivity are helping position travel as a critical path to opening our hearts and minds to culture, history, and people.

The Transformative Travel Council defines transformational travel as, "Intentionally traveling to stretch, learn and grow into new ways of being and engaging with the world".

Another perspective might be as simple as giving people something to look forward to. The idea of healthy anticipation is no longer a trivial matter; the pandemic has impacted people's mental health. According to a study done by the Government of Ontario, many have seen their stress level double since the pandemic began and as many as 7 out of 10 people believe we are heading for a mental health crisis.*

The key is to position the vacation or trip as something much bigger than the trip itself. It is to elevate the importance of the trip so that it takes up a place of reverence in their lives.

If the trip could speak, it would say to your client, *"We are doing this, no matter what!"*.

Increasing your unique selling proposition

Anyone can sell an all-inclusive resort or a cruise. At one time, they were considered complex. However, with the combined sophistication of technology and the growing comfort of high-end online purchases, in today's market, you need to stand out by making the booking complex.

The more value you can add to the sale, the more unique you are.

Chapter Summary
10X Commerce: Earn More Money in Less Time

- Positioning travel perks as purely incremental, helps ensure you are getting paid your full value on the work you do for your clients.

- Selling at a higher price point may be harder at face value but less competition, more need for advice, and a much higher total compensation make a compelling argument for becoming highly skilled at it.

- The lion's share of your commercial strategy starts and ends with your ability to close the sale.

- Investing in a preplanned discovery conversation with a set agenda and a plethora of thought-provoking questions is one of the best ways to improve your chances of closing the sale.

- The research shows that since the pandemic, there has been a sharp increase in advisors who charge fees. While fees vary depending on the scope of travel planning required, one thing is clear: advisors who charge fees earn more.

- Fees are your cue that you are working with a buyer (rather than a shopper).

- Luxury travel is the fastest growing segment of the travel industry. According to Luxury Travel Magazine, it's growing one third faster than any other segment.

- Upselling is an integrated approach to positioning price and value that can double, or even triple the amount a client is willing to invest upfront in their vacation.

- People buy with their hearts and justify with their heads.

- The only way to know whether something is truly out of budget for a client is to explore it with them.

- Dabbling in luxury is available to everyone. It is the "masstige" approach to selling (mass market with prestige options).

- Effectively positioning the value of travel through fluency, the freedom to choose, and upgrading the fixed options is the key to becoming more commercially successful.

Points to Ponder

- How much do travel perks factor into your view of your compensation?

- How might they be getting in the way of your commercial success?

- Considering the lion's share of your success depends on your ability to close the sale. How much time do you spend investing in improving your skills here?

- How might charging or increasing your fees improve the quality of your client relationships?

- Do you have a list of pre-planned discovery questions? How could improving them increase your closing and upselling successes?

- How do you plan on leveraging the increased demand for luxury travel?

- How might you introduce luxury "dabbling" or "masstige travel"?

- Which products are you most comfortable presenting the luxury option for? Why?

Chapter 7

10X Impact — Part One
Making a Difference: To
be Transformational is
Priceless

We are in a different stream. Unlike the salmon returning home, we can't go back to where we were before. And we can't move forward without knowing exactly where we are and where we want to get to.

Over and over, I've heard advisors say, *"I'm done. I'm tired of all the changes. I still love the travel industry but I want to come back differently than before. I want things to be BETTER!"*

Yes, you can come back better. No one deserves it more than you. This is YOUR time to make an impact!

You've come from the worst possible place. Through no fault of your own, you hit rock bottom. However, moving out of rock bottom is completely within your control.

Making an impact in the world starts with considering where you are currently, and where you want to be in the future.

It also involves considering of where your customers are coming from. Sometimes, our customers and their frustrations impact how we feel.

The following chart reviews each of these stages, along with the customer impact, and tips for achieving a 10X transformation.

Value Model

Impact	How you feel	How clients feel	Loyalty
Transformation	Indispensable	Devoted	10X
Trusted	Invincible	Excited	5X
Testing	Confident	Relieved	1X
Transactional	Worn out	Demanding	Zero
Train Wreck	Despondent	Desperate	- 10X

Trainwreck

This is a rock-bottom place in your business. It's where you feel like giving up.

In March of 2020, the world stopped traveling. We were in a collective freefall. Not one human being on earth had ever experienced anything like it. No one knew the extent of what we were dealing with, nor did anyone know where rock bottom was.

In hindsight, we were right to be terrified. We were right to stop everything in favour of looking after the people closest to us, as well as ourselves.

We can laugh now at disinfecting our groceries, or the mad rush for toilet paper. We can smile at the banana bread baking bonanza (to this day I'm having a hard time working up an interest in eating it again).

Not even the brightest among scientists, doctors or economists could have predicted the depth of the impact the pandemic would have on our industry.

It still feels at times like unless you are in the travel industry you really have no idea how hard it has been.

There have been multiple rock-bottom moments for us, including:

- Canada banning cruise ships

- The new Delta variant

- CDC increasing the level four advisory against cruise ships

- December Omicron outbreak.

It was January 2022. Omicron was blowing up, lockdowns were back in place, and suddenly there was a deafening silence. The financial impact of losing peak holiday travel revenue, the devastation of the seasonal boom of bookings, and the virus itself was like a tornado of destruction sweeping through the travel industry.

During this period, I continued to make calls to advisors to check in with their emotional state and the state of their business.

"I'm done! I'm done! I'm done!"

Those words were painful to hear. Most expressed these words in the agony of the moment, and they would show resilience by coming back to fight another day.

How Clients Feel — Desperate

The entire world is running on empty. Even when you're having a good day, you can be managing someone who is not.

There are signs everywhere:

When you are in a trainwreck state, your clients feel desperate and may even lash out. There were advisors who experienced travel shaming.

Clients may be viewing your attempt to restart your business as irresponsible because they are desperate, and simply not ready to embrace travel.

The Key to Changing State

The key point is to recognize when you are in this state. That is the trainwreck, "I'm done", I-simply-cannot-on state.

What got you there? More importantly, what should you do to recover? Take this advice from leading psychologist Sean Grover LCSW:

"Don't get right back up.

*When you're viciously knocked down by life, **don't get right back up**. Like tripping and falling, you have the impulse to rise and start moving again. But ignoring a serious injury will make it worse.*

Pain demands attention; it needs to be acknowledged and embraced before you can move on."

This advice is especially hard for high achievers to take. Time and time again, since the beginning of the pandemic, you've thrown yourself into continued learning.

You've tried to replace the pace you used to know of running a busy travel business by attending webinars, calling clients, and trying to get the world traveling again.

All of those things are important, in due course. But when your life feels like a trainwreck, moving on too quickly is a coping mechanism.

When our daughter Gillian was born, we had a real challenge figuring out how to help her get to sleep.

She was awake day and night, and never seemed to want to close her eyes. I would rock her, walk around the house with her, put her in the stroller or the car... I even tried to hypnotize her by dramatically closing my eyes really close to hers!

When she finally succumbed to sleep, putting her down would wake her up and she'd start crying all over again. She loved being awake!

I remember when I hit rock bottom. She hadn't slept for more than two hours at a time for weeks on end.

I was sitting on the stairs in our den at three in the morning. She was crying, I was sobbing. I felt like a *complete* failure as a mother.

I went to visit our doctor for our 12-week check-up with deep circles under my eyes. I had read all the books and our beautiful daughter was simply not following any of the "normal" sleeping patterns.

The doctor, who was a highly sought-after paediatrician and a magnificent human being, sat me down and started asking about how I was getting by.

She coached me with ideas on how to get support so that I would get enough sleep to deal with the challenge of a very alert, bright, and beautiful baby girl.

"Don't believe everything you read. Some babies don't need a lot of sleep! She'll figure it out and then once she does get sleep, look out world!" she chuckled.

She taught me how to help Gillian soothe herself to sleep by putting her to bed in a happy, awake state.

Knowing how to soothe yourself is the art of stabilizing yourself and your business when you are in a state of disarray.

Taking time out by going on a trip or getting away for an extended period of time is essential. However, it is not the answer. In fact, it can be even more destabilizing.

Have you ever noticed that sometimes your deepest frustration appears shortly after you've returned from a vacation? The magic you felt when you were away only seemed to exaggerate how bad things are going for you back home.

It's the daily ritual of soothing yourself that provides long-term stability to your mental health and well-being.

Meditation, working in shorter bursts, and adding more self-development to your work are all critical components to sustaining long-term joy.

Transactional

This way this time, that way next time, another way another time.

Transactional relationships lack both depth and continuity. They therefore leave no room for improvement in efficiency over long periods of time.

Every customer gets a slightly different experience, but their experiences are not identical in areas they could be.

Take something as simple as an email. We send hundreds, if not thousands of very similar emails. Lately, we've been sending more of the "checking in" emails, but at other times we might send emails for upsell opportunities or a final payment. The point is, we send a lot of emails that are similar in nature.

Creating a draft email for suppliers, customers or colleagues, that opens and closes in a similar way, can save you an hour a week. That's 52 hours per year!

When you are operating in transactional mode, you are in survival mode. You're not taking the time to simplify and aggregate your activities.

When you are in a transactional mode with clients, you act as if this will probably be the only time you ever book them. You realize — either by your own omission or by the way the booking has transpired — that you lack depth of understanding in your relationship with them.

The result over time is exhaustion and burnout.

How Clients Feel

When you don't know a client well, or you disagree with their approach to working with you, they can seem demanding.

It's true, clients can be downright demanding, especially in a Covid and travel world where it's hard to find answers. According to Answer the Public, here are the top five questions being searched online:

- Where do I get tests?

- What tests do I need?

- When will testing be dropped?

- Where can I get advice?

- What insurance do I need?

When someone asks you which test they need, you wonder what rock they've been hiding under; did they miss the memo that the world is having a pandemic?

However, when clients are demanding, you have the greatest opportunity to earn their trust.

The Key to Changing State

The key to changing state from transactional to transformational is to start by understanding your new role.

Specifically, in order to help clients buy better, consider the customer buying-cycle pre- and post-pandemic.

The Two Customer Buying Cycles

In the past, this was the customer buying cycle:

Consider the new customer buying cycle which has one
additional step: keeping your customer calm.

In the past, people would dream about travel, ask a few trip-
related questions, and then begin with travel planning.

After a good discovery session, you would qualify the
customer and uncover needs. Then you would move the client
from dreaming to planning by presenting three options.

Since the pandemic began there has been a new step in
the cycle where every traveler must come to terms with the
rules, regulations, and process of adding Covid testing to
their trip.

Rest assured, I understand that after two long years of Covid conversations, I'm sure you'd rather do just about anything rather than bring up Covid. However, it is essential.

If you skip this step, you are more vulnerable to the trip unravelling and cancelling.

Even if you get the client clear on the new rules and regulations, when they return home with news of the trip to their traveling companion, the companion's questions erode the traveler's confidence in their decision to move forward.

Your job is to stay calm and help buyers cross the bridge of confusion between dreaming and planning.

Establishing The Calm Stage

W.A.I.T stands for "Why Am I Talking?".

It's a reminder that when a client approaches you in an agitated state or uncertain mindset, rather than jumping into advisor-knows-best mode, stop, stay calm, and ask a question.

The two best questions you can ask at this stage are:

- What has your research told you so far?

- What do you know about Covid and travel?

These questions get the client to open up and speak from the heart. You must listen carefully and without judgement.

You are the advocate of safe travel. Before you can propose safe travel options, you need a keen understanding of their individual perspective.

Another important aspect of the calm state is that everyone who is traveling needs to be present.

To be clear, this is not new since Covid, and likely was part of your planning stage prior to the pandemic. It has always been best practice to give anyone whose needs must be taken care of during the trip, the opportunity to share those needs directly with you.

Going forward, it is especially important to have all travelers present in order to clarify a sense of calm decision making for all.

The mistake agents make is thinking that one person has a clear understanding of the other's needs.

Recently, an agent shared a "trainwreck" of an experience, where a group leader had insisted that she be the only person who spoke for the group.

This might sound tempting at first, however, all too soon the booking became a nightmare as one by one the individuals began reaching out with their individual preferences. These were not in line at all with what had been requested for them.

"What they wanted was perfectly reasonable months ago, and prior to the pandemic when suppliers were more accessible. However, travel has exploded and wait times are endless. Now I can't even deliver the slightest change."

The bottom line? Stay calm, and ensure every traveler is heard.

How Clients Feel

Once you begin to see your role as an ambassador to the new buyer's journey, complete with a sense of calm, clients will feel the much-needed reassurance they need that they've made the right decision to travel.

The Key to Changing State

The key to moving away from a transactional state is understanding where your clients are in their journey.

Your role is to help them move through the journey with a sense of calm and confidence.

Testing

In the testing stage, you are optimizing the questions you've asked and testing the boundaries of creativity and design.

You are also testing the boundaries of travel experiences and investment levels.

Your discovery conversations clarify expectations, giving you the freedom and flexibility to go to work for your clients.

Think of it as a science experiment. For an experiment to be a success it must have three things:

① A hypothesis. In the testing phase, your hypothesis is that you have a better way for your clients to experience this trip.

② The controlled set. The controlled set is based on a keen discovery process. You listen for clues about on what exactly they are asking for.

③ The changed set. This is the impact of your service and your creativity.

In order to know the impact you have on your clients, you need to fully understand their core needs.

In other words, to exceed expectations, you must first meet them.

For example,

① Your hypothesis: Adding a luxury option every time you present to clients will increase your luxury sales.

② A control set: This is what they've asked for. You prepare this option based on the discovery questions.

A changed set: Offer what they've asked for, a 'slight stretch' version, and a luxury option each time.

Measure the difference between the single product offered and the result of offering luxury every time.

There are many different things you can do in the testing phase to help clients get much more out of their experience of working with you.

How Clients Feel

A client who is an active participant in your testing phase feels both excited and relieved. They feel heard and appreciate that you care as much about their vacation as they do.

To be on the other side of options that introduce a better way to travel is like winning the lottery for your clients.

When you are running the show and pushing boundaries on their behalf, it's exciting to them!

"Step so far out of your comfort zone you forget how to get back."

~ Unknown

The Key to Changing State

When you are in the testing phase, you gain confidence in your ability to deliver an outstanding sales and service experience.

Look back on the conversion and commercial strategies.

Choose any one of dozens of marketing, selling, and servicing techniques.

Spend thirty days testing novel ways of enhancing the customer experience of working with you.

Trusted

Once you've established the best practices during the testing state, there is an important and altogether underestimated shift from testing to trusted.

- Testing is going through the motions of doing the right things.

- Trusted moves you into doing things for the right people and for the right reasons.

The tagline of becoming a trusted advisor is one of the most used and often misused in the travel industry.

- Trust is the basis of every relationship.

- It takes time and effort on both sides to establish trust.

- Trust can be broken in an instant.

- Perceived trust and earned trust are vastly different.

In his book, *Speed of Trust*, Stephen M.R. Covey outlines the 13 trust behaviours we use as our compass.

The values themselves are not surprising; they include long-term views, commitments, honesty, and transparency.

What is surprising is the massive gap between how we view ourselves and how we view others.

Speed of trust comparison

Value	How I View Myself	How I View Others
Results	84.25	51.5
Capabilities	78.10	55.2
Intent	88.77	58.4
Integrity	95.45	59.6
Listen First	86.5	58.1
Right Wrongs	95.8	58.1
Confront Reality	86.6	58.4
Create Transparency	96.1	58.6

The reason, he explains, is that most of us are familiar with how trust feels. It's comforting when we have it, and extremely uncomfortable when we don't.

In order to close the gap, we need to consider trust as a verb. In order to feel trust, we need to create trust.

Consider the top three values of results, integrity, and intent.

1. Results with clients: you provided what was asked for and delivered it in such a way that they would rate you high on results.

2. Integrity: you did what you said you would do. You acted with True North principles. No one was spoken to unkindly, harassed, demeaned, or cheated on.

3. Intent: this is your motives and behaviors. When you are transparent about your motives and your boundaries, it helps clarify expectations.

Delivering on expectations is paramount to trust. So is creating expectations. Clients need to be trained on how to be a good client for you.

For example, there's no sense in getting frustrated when a client books direct if you haven't explained to them that they will be bombarded with other offers as soon as they book.

How Clients Feel

Clients feel that they are entering a trusted relationship. They are starting to feel a deep sense of appreciation for what you are doing, as if above and beyond is the only way you work.

The Key to Changing State

Trust is a lofty goal. It takes tremendous effort and can easily be broken. In order to move from testing to trusted, follow two simple rules.

1. **Only work at a pace that allows you to be trustworthy.**
    We don't intentionally let people down. If we miss a deadline or over promise and under deliver, it's not how we started out.

    Falling short on delivery is most often a case of being overwhelmed and overworked.

2. **Only work with people you enjoy.**
    It's a choice to move slower and to build trust with every customer you work with. Your intention is to become MY travel advisor.

    In my book, Flying Colours, I dedicate an entire chapter to The Customer Shift. This customer shift means you stop being all things to all people, and start being indispensable to one ideal customer at a time.

Transformational

Here, the journey takes a distinct turn in the form of a life-changing impact for both you and your clients.

A transformational level of delivery is in complete alignment with your purpose. You are doing your best work. The relationship has elevated you from travel advisor to travel guru, mentor, or trusted advisor in every sense of the word.

You are confident in your discovery of what matters most in the world to your clients when they are traveling, and when they are not.

You know your worth and you are getting paid accordingly.

Transformation focuses on creating change for good.

It requires a deep understanding of what problems clients are seeking to solve. When you have asked the right questions and developed rapport, you begin to understand the meaning of the trip in the big picture of their life's journey.

You also know what changes they would like to see in themselves before, during, and after the trip.

What would it mean to you to create a life-changing impact on someone not by just the trip itself but by the way the trip was delivered?

To be transformational is to be priceless.

How Clients Feel

Clients who are now treated as transformational clients feel devoted to you. You will hear words like 'above and beyond', 'the extra mile', and 'always there'.

Transformational clients demonstrate their devotion to you through loyalty and advocacy. They make it clear they would not leave home without out you.

They also refer their friends and colleagues at an extraordinary level. One advisor wrote, *"I can trace back $1 million in referral sales to a single client"*.

The Key to Maintaining This State

Coming out of the pandemic, people are craving a transformation. Travel can help us open our hearts and minds to a greater life, even with Covid in it.

You have the opportunity to create a transformation through travel. The impact of your work is far greater than you know.

Now that you have the scope for moving from a trainwreck state to a transformational one, you need a strategy to execute.

This strategy allows you to keep climbing towards a transformational state, even when there are setbacks.

It's called the 10X impact strategy.

The 10X Impact Strategy

In the first chapter, we revealed the framework to 10X your travel business based on purpose, people, process, and performance.

This framework is your True North. It's based on your values of doing work you love with people you enjoy working with.

There's a saying: if you love what you do, you'll never work a day in your life.

I think it's safe to say that, at least for a period of time, rebuilding your travel business is going to feel like work. Doing work on purpose, in a way that brings you joy is going to make it all the more worthwhile.

The key is to focus on your process in order to keep the climb up Comeback Mountain as efficient as possible.

So far, we've reviewed three strategies for improving our climb:

1. **Connection strategy:**
   To capture and nurture high-value customers through connection.

2. **Conversion strategy:**
   To create a steady stream of high-value customers through attraction, retention, and upskilling.

3. **Commercial strategy:**
   To increase revenue per transaction through selling, upselling, cross selling, and fees.

Now let's review the impact strategy.

This one is slightly different than the other three in that it's not based on anyone but you. All three of the previous strategies related to your ability to create customers and keep them for life. While customers are critical to your business, and indeed the reason for your business, this final strategy is all about you:

4. **Impact strategy:**
   To make an impact in the world and on others through your commitment to excellence and making your dreams come true.

To make an impact in the world, you need a dream. You need an idea of the kind of life that brings you joy. We spend a great deal of time thinking, worrying, and even obsessing about what is not working.

We look back at past problems that bring regrets, frustration, and anger, or we dwell on our roadblocks. Instead of making a decision and moving on, we get stuck in indecision.

The National Bureau of Sciences says that 80 per cent of our thoughts are repeated and 95 per cent of them are negative.

It's no wonder that dreaming or even knowing what you want in life does not come naturally.

We are predisposed to shut down our own possibility mindset.

Making an impact comes from a deep and passionate commitment to being your best and helping others. In order to achieve this, you must have a commitment to your dream. The ability to make a 10X impact is dependent on your commitment to excellence.

Let's explore these ideas in order to help you make your impact in the world.

Commitment to Your Dream

Your vision of yourself being ten times bigger, better, and bolder than before has a tremendous impact on your ability to start the 10X journey.

The traditional method of goalsetting is to come up with a big number: *"I want to sell X million dollars"*.

The expectation is that the number alone should be enough to motivate you.

Dan Sullivan's idea that 10X is easier than 2X makes sense on paper. Yet, there is a disconnect between the number and the execution.

Dan emphasizes the need for you to fully commit to the idea that you *can* grow by ten times.

In order to build the belief that you can grow your travel business 10X, you need to make it extremely attractive by creating a vision with vivid details.

A vision is a motion picture of your dreams. You are the director. Achieving extraordinary results is far easier when you have a clear picture of what extraordinary looks like in every area of your life.

My Extraordinary Life

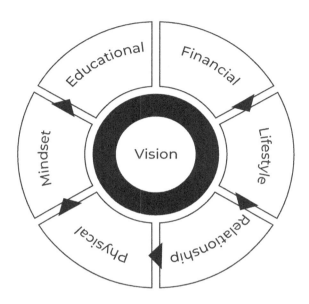

Expanding the ideas for your life helps you fill in more details.

- Financial — A dream of financial independence, freedom, and wealth.

- Lifestyle — This is your work/life balance. Picture how many days of work and how many days of play you might have. Include what your ideal play days look like.

- Relationships — Who will you serve? Relationships include those with clients, friends, family, and your community.

- Physical — All of the details that pertain to your health, from regular checkups to healthy eating and exercise.

- Mindset: An intentional disposition to create a positive state of mind.

- Education: Personal growth and development to become all you can be.

The Gift of Not Measuring Up

There are two important gifts in not measuring up. The gift of identifying the gap, and the gift of "So what?".

In his book, *The Compound Effect,* Darren Hardy wrote a vision of everything he wanted in a future wife. He wrote pages and pages of vivid detail.

When he looked at what he wanted, he realized that in no way would this epic vision of a partner be attracted to who he was at the time.

The hidden benefit of not measuring up to the vision we have for our life is that it unveils a very important insight: the gap.

What you want and *getting what you want* are only separated by one thing: the experience of having achieved it.

Achievement is, therefore, simply having the skills to get something done.

For each area of your life, where do you gave a gap between what you want and what you have?

When I considered becoming an author, I was very focused on the fact that I had never written a book before.

I was filled with the imposter syndrome, right down to the English professor in university who told me I was nothing short of incompetent.

Once I had written my first book, I realized I had everything I needed to write a book. The gap vanished.

A perfect unpublished book is nowhere near as helpful as a less-than-perfect book out in the world.

Knowing that perfect is an impossible standard (that you will never measure up to) is also a gift.

The second gift is the gift of being able to ask "Who cares?" and let go of your need to be perfect in doing so.

I highly recommend Lynn Cazaly's book, *Ish*, to anyone who struggles with the imposter syndrome or perfectionism.

Lynn writes:

"In choosing to push towards perfection I gained nothing and missed out on nearly everything."

How to Make an Impact

To make an impact in the world, you don't need money, a title, popularity, or followers. You don't need material possessions such as cars, houses, or even trips, though they can be part of your dream to the extent that they keep you motivated.

To make an impact in the world, you only need two things: a special talent, and to share that talent with others.

You make an impact — consciously or not — every day, especially in travel.

Perhaps a trip you planned for someone saved a marriage that went on to produce a beautiful family. Maybe it's a milestone birthday trip that turns out to be their last.

It's hard to put a value on what you do, but it is essential that you recognize it. Impact is the greatest reward of all.

The day you discover the special way you make a difference to others, and decide to do so in a bigger way, is really the day you find your purpose.

There is a beautiful Indian proverb:

"Blessed is he who plants trees under whose shade he will never sit."

When you believe that what you do matters, you want to get better at it. The first step towards making your dreams come true is for you to believe that you can.

Your Special Talent

Making an impact is directly tied to your unique ability. Every single person has a special talent that helps shape who they are. That talent, when shared with others, makes a difference to them.

- You don't have to look far to recognize your special talent, but it may come so naturally to you that you don't realize that it is unique.

- Your special talent is what sets you apart from every other person.

- Your family loves you for it. It gets called out by customers, friends, and even people you've just met.

- Your special talent is so intriguing to you that you might spend hours getting better and better at it.

- Your special talent is at the core of making a 10X impact.

Time spent getting ten times better at your special talent will get you to the top of Comeback Mountain in half the time.

The 'I Am' Statement — Believing in YOU!

There is abundant research on the connection between conceiving ideas, believing in those ideas, and achieving them. As Napoleon Hill famously said:

> *"Whatever the mind can conceive and believe, it can achieve."*

For those of you who, like me, had a hard time buying into the "I am" philosophy, my experience with it has been enlightening and helpful. Here is what I've learned.

The science behind the "I am" statement is that the brain cannot differentiate between what is real and what is imagined.

It also does not want you to be out of alignment, therefore it seeks information to back up whatever message you are sending. The classic example of this is when you're thinking about buying a car and, suddenly, you see them everywhere.

Creating "I am" statements for your life conditions your brain to seek positive inputs that make those statements reality for you.

When you begin every day with an "I am" statement such as "I am healthy", "I am strong", or "I am enough", the day takes on that as your core belief. It alters your mindset from a future or desired state to a present state.

For the rest of the day, you are on a mission to achieve it, without doing anything.

If that isn't enough, it's a truth that has stood the test of time. In 1637, Descartes wrote:

"I think therefore I am."

Mobilizing Thoughts into Ideas, and Ideas into Action

Every dream needs a symbol, a big word, or powerful quote to mobilize thoughts into ideas and ideas into action. These powerful icons provide context and act as powerful reminders of everything you're trying to achieve.

When I write the words **"Comeback Mountain"**, I visualize my mission to help mobilize the travel industry. We cannot go back to the old mountain. I see a new mountain of opportunity ahead.

In his TED Talk (based on his best-selling book, *Think Again)*, Adam Grant tells a powerful story about a climbing trip he and his friends took in Panama. Their goal was to hike to see a volcano.

The hike was supposed to take two hours. After four hours, they knew something was amiss.

They kept climbing, clinging to the hope that they were wrong whilst instinctively knowing they were right. They were way off course but refused to turn back.

After six long hours, they were exhausted, and eventually they had to be airlifted out.

The reason they did not turn back, he explains, is something called, "Escalation of commitment to a losing action". It's what happens when you don't walk away from an investment or a slot machine.

I think of that story in my own life. I've been so committed to the idea of a goal or a career that I ignored all the warning signs that I was no longer climbing the right mountain for me.

The goal of this book, and my deepest hope for you, is that you will focus on a new and better way forward.

I keep a photo in my office as a reminder of my mission to help the industry up Comeback Mountain. This is the actual photo I use to remind me of which mountain I'm climbing.

The one in the back may be taller, but the sun is always on my face if I stay focused on enjoying the journey.

"A big word is also a very useful tool for creating a context for a bigger goal.
A big word is a helpful framework for giving context to your priorities.
Picking a word of the year can bring clarity and focus to whom we want to become and what we want to accomplish in life. A carefully chosen word is a type of mental mentor — something to help us stay motivated as we move toward our goals."

~ Robyn Flanigan

Your big word is code for everything you're trying to achieve. It reminds you of why you are on this mission. It helps you decide what you want to celebrate.

Your big word is a way to measure meaningful success.

My big word this year is "elevate". I want to elevate how others experience me, whether it's through coaching, mentoring, or writing, so that I have the maximum impact on their work and lives. It motivates me to keep learning, trying, failing, and trying again.

I've also had "breakthrough", "curious", and "rise up" in recent years. I can look back on each of those years and see the progress I made based on that context.

Skilling Up
The skill of learning new skills.

We know that the secret to a thriving travel business is to be excellent at what you do. The most successful advisors get known, recommended, and referred based on their level of expertise.

This profound level of capability, in turn, increases your commitment to the dream.

What you may not know is how imperative the skill of learning new skills will be in the future.

First, consider the new stream that you are swimming in. It is the stream that has the pandemic in it.

In the past, finding, converting, and engaging clients had a consistent flow to it. As travel rules relax, and with each positive announcement, the demand floods in and the need for new skills rises.

World cruises and new program releases are selling out in hours. Suppliers have transformed their products dramatically since Covid, and they continue to modify the experiences to adjust to local safety protocols and new consumer preferences.

In the meantime, marketing, sales, and technology have vastly accelerated over the past two years.

The use and acceptance of digital marketing have exploded. You can leave video messages, send digital proposals, book, invoice, and manage all of your appointments on free or almost free platforms that barely existed before we began our two-year hiatus.

In addition to all the changes since the pandemic, the sheer volume of new products, new technologies, and both rising demand and "demands" from consumers is staggering.

All of this requires you to learn new skills at scale so that you can not only keep up, but get ahead of it and capitalize on the massive opportunity.

Learning a new skill is a 2X concept; learning how you learn so you can learn faster and learn new things more often without losing your way is a 10X concept. That is called *skilling up,* and it is the superpower of the post-pandemic travel era.

Here are five key steps to moving from learning a new skill (2X) to learning how to learn faster by skilling up (10X).

Step #1: Assess to Start

The best way to learn a new skill is to start with an honest assessment of where you are now.

According to renowned entrepreneur and self-development guru, Dan Sullivan, "All progress starts by telling the truth".

What skill or skills are you missing to get you to the next level?

To go up a level, what skills are needed in each of the key areas of your business?

Here are a few areas to consider: communication, strategy, decision making, connecting to customers (marketing), sales, finance, and productivity (time management).

Step #2: Focus Fosters Faster Learning

If you place a magnifying glass on dry kindling at the right temperature, you can start a fire in less than a minute.

Focus on learning a new skill with the right level of intensity, using the right tools and the best resources. You will create an energy that is both precise and powerful.

> *"Concentrate all your thoughts upon the work at hand.*
> *The sun's rays do not burn until brought to a focus."*
> *~ **Alexander Graham Bell***

Focus with frequency and cadence. In the next chapter, we'll explore how monthly skill-sprints can enhance your ability to get to the next level.

Step #3: Learning Leads to Power

Knowledge is power. Knowing how to do something can change everything about how you take on new challenges.

Not knowing holds power over you and keeps you in a place of fear.

That is why the journey to knowledge is an important one. Learning how to learn new skills makes you more confident and powerful.

Learning a new skill allows you to save time, money, and resources. Here are five tips for faster learning:

1.   Know how you learn best.

2.   Read the manual.

3.   Find a friend who already knows how.

4.   Start small, start fast.

5.   Teach others.

Step #4: Test by Doing

What evidence do you have that you are making progress in learning a new skill? It doesn't come from reading books, watching endless YouTube videos or scanning the internet.

Often, when we decide we're going to tackle a new skill, we dive into Google and YouTube, hoping for the perfect match to: "How to (insert skill)".

After hours of search-engine hell, we start asking (or begging) around for someone to do it for us. We either give up or spend a fortune trying to get the right resource.

The only way to test for progress is to get messy with it. Get out there and just do it! You might make a mess of it on your first try. I cringe at some of my early newsletters and social media posts. It's hard to put yourself out there! However, positive feedback and a bit of good luck will keep you going. and soon you'll be at the next level.

Here's the good news about the skill journey: improving on a skill is much easier than adopting a new skill. You're only a beginner once.

Step #5: Sprint to Finish

It's commonly believed that it takes 21 days to create a habit. However, that seems to be a myth.

According to Phillippa Lally, a health psychology researcher at University College London, a new habit usually takes a little more than two months — 66 days to be exact — and as many as 254 days until it's fully formed.

In other words, it depends! So, choose a time frame that is long enough to make an impact but short enough for you to stay engaged.

In my book, *Flying Colours*, I created a framework to help you achieve new skills and habits every 30 days. We'll delve deeper into developing new habits later in the book.

Taking on a new skill is exciting! Skilling up by learning how to learn is life changing.

Chapter Summary
10X Impact — Part One
Making a Difference: To be Transformational is Priceless

- Making an impact in the world starts with considering where you are currently, and where you want to be in the future. There are five states between trainwreck and transformation:

  - Trainwreck: The entire world is running on empty. Even when you're having a good day, you can be managing someone who is not.

  - Transactional: These relationships lack depth and continuity, enabling no room for improvement in efficiency.

  - Testing: Enjoying the benefits of trying new strategies for improved performance over time.

  - Trust: Only work at a pace that allows you to be trustworthy.

  - Transformational: The relationship has elevated you from travel advisor to travel guru, mentor, or trusted advisor.

- Impact strategy means making an impact in the world and on others through your commitment to excellence in everything you do.

- Your vision of yourself being ten times bigger, better, and bolder than before has a tremendous impact on your ability to start the 10X journey.

- Creating "I am" statements for your life conditions your brain to seek positive inputs that make those statements reality for you.

- A big word is a helpful framework for giving context to your priorities.

- Learning a new skill is a 2X concept. Learning how to learn faster so you can learn new things more often is a 10X concept called skilling up.

- There are five stages of skilling up:

  - Assess to start

  - Focus fosters faster learning

  - Learning leads to power

  - Test by doing

  - Sprint to the finish.

Points to Ponder

- Where do you see yourself currently in your journey from trainwreck to transformation?

- What happens when you slide backwards on your journey?

- What does excellence mean to you? How do you define it?

- What is your vision for yourself three years from now?

- If you were to send a message back to your current self from your future self, what would it say?

- What "I am" statements can you create for yourself that would be a positive affirmation of vision?

- What is your big word?

- What quotes, sayings or symbols do you have that represent the context of your vision?

- What new skills do you need that you don't currently have to achieve your vision?

- What benefits do you see in the post-pandemic era to learning how to learn faster (skilling up)?

Chapter 8

10X Impact — Part Two: Executing the Dream

I want to end on a high note. How to craft the perfect day — every day!

The perfect day is the gateway to getting everything you want.

It's the ideal container size to put your ideas about productivity, pacing, and performance into practice. It allows you to make a game of it!

When I first started my "perfect day" journey, I was fresh out of overwhelm. I had just left a job that consumed me from the moment I woke up in the morning until I collapsed on my pillow at night.

I had back-to-back-to-back meetings every single day. I delivered over 250 presentations a year to audiences of 2 to 2000.

As the SVP for a large travel company, who had trouble with setting boundaries, my day was a hot mess. They were often ten-hour days with a two-hour commute.

When I left, I had an initial burst of excitement and energy; I finally had time to think! I took courses, learned new skills, and started a brand-new business, all at the young age of 57!

More importantly, I learned how to make massive improvements to my productivity simply by creating the ideal environment to support how *I* get things done.

I am now ten times better at knowing myself and holding myself accountable in pursuit of my goals. I've accomplished more in the past three years than I did in the entire previous decade.

I remember thinking, "What a shame I didn't learn these skills on how to approach the day while I was in the whirlwind of the busy corporate world".

Every single human beings needs to work at a pace that allows them to be their best self.

Looking back, I wondered how I could create a system that would have saved the old me, and would help others like me.

If you're a go getter who loves what you do and has a strong work ethic, yet you have trouble "switching off", then this approach to work will be a tremendous help.

Or maybe you're not sure what you really want, so you drift through the days and weeks, wondering where the time went?

I have clients who are working 70-hour weeks. When the going gets tough, busy, or overly demanding, they find themselves wasting time that they don't have. They procrastinate, which only makes things worse.

The secret to becoming ten times better is to pay attention to the way you work, as much as the work itself.

The Approach Is the Work

The biggest lesson I learned about how to be massively productive was a profound one.

I learned that the approach is not more important or less important than the work. The approach IS the work.

What do I mean by that?

The way you carry out your role, interact with clients, complete proposals, or do just about anything, is the sum total of the work you do.

It's easy to think that the result or the outcome is the work. In actual fact, the result is a culmination of your dreams, pressures, intentions, fears, procrastination, skills, and habits.

As Dr. Benjamin Hardy says,

"The way you do anything is the way you do everything."

I suddenly realized that it was okay to put time into my mindset. I could take long walks in the middle of my day. I learned that putting the timer on to set limits on how long I worked at certain tasks improved my energy levels.

I paid attention to how I felt on days where I was in front of the computer, compared to days where I had a high level of human interaction.

Not only is it okay; focusing on your inner self to ground your day is essential to your mental health and wellbeing.

I took time to put everything I ever wanted out in front of me. More time off, more balance, less stress.

I still wanted to achieve big dreams. I want a thriving coaching practice, to write a book a year for five years, and to speak in front of large audiences about how to become ten times better in half the time.

I couldn't *not* want to achieve. However, I'm learning *how* to achieve by focusing on how I achieve.

That is what the perfect day is all about: finding new ways to grow ten times better in half the time in a way that works for you.

We are all different. Some people are morning people; some work better late at night. Some of us get energy talking to people; others find themselves exhausted after a long conversation or meeting.

Once you begin to notice your natural rhythms, and you align those rhythms with your purpose, along with the work that needs to get done to fulfill it, a new world of productivity opens up to you.

The approach is the work.

Let's get started!

The Perfect Day Is Like Baking a Cake!

The perfect day is a set period of time in which you work on your priorities and tasks towards your big goal at a pace that brings you joy and balance.

If the perfect day was a cake recipe, the individual tasks and priorities would be the ingredients and method, and the big goal would be the cake!

The essential ingredients of tasks, priorities and goals all work together to create the foundation of your day.

It is unlikely you'll bake your whole cake in a day, but the more you can work on priorities rather than smaller tasks, or tablespoons rather than teaspoons, the more progress you'll make.

Skills would be the liquid that binds the cake together. Skills accelerate the outcome. It's impossible to make the cake without them.

Habits would be the baking powder that helps the cake rise. Your habits elevate your performance.

Mix this recipe at the pace of a wooden spoon rather than an electric beater. At times, we need to beat rapidly, but when we add too much speed, we overmix and burn out.

Bake at the right temperature. Take breaks in the day for fresh air, warm connections, and a good laugh.

Most of all, indulge in the magnificent cake you've created by enjoying it with family and friends. Cake should never be eaten alone!

Your friends are the network of people who make it all worthwhile. They are also there to watch your mastery take shape and to give you the odd bit of cooking advice, even when you don't need it!

Priorities: The Do List

Priorities are groups of tasks that, when done consistently, will make the biggest impact on your business.

Priorities help you narrow the never-ending list of things you *could do* into what you *must do*. They separate the unimportant tasks from the important ones.

Priorities allow you to create the do list, rather than the to-do list.

Instead of creating a to-do list with dozens of tasks, prioritize a group of those tasks to ensure progress is made towards your biggest goal.

They are specific and measurable, with a date attached.

Here are a few examples of the difference between general tasks and specific priorities.

General Task	Priority
Call my database.	Make 100 calls by March 31st. Reconnect with every past client to assess their readiness to travel by March 31st.
Sell more luxury.	Complete the Seabourn Academy by June 1st. Offer luxury to every client for the next 60 days.
Read more.	Read three books on growing my business by March 31st. Finish 10X My Travel Business by July 1st.
Increase my social media.	Create a 12-week content repository and post three times a week. Start my new Luxury Facebook Group by May 1st.

The Wooden Spoon Pace

As a former long-distance runner, I know the value of pacing myself on race day. Typically, whether it's a 10K race or a marathon, the adrenaline rush at the starting line is impossible to ignore.

You start the race, feeling the runners beside you, and your feet naturally start moving faster and faster. This produces a lovely rush of endorphins to your brain and suddenly you feel like you could run forever.

You soon learn that even the slightest increase above your conditioning level will leave you feeling like you have cement in your shoes in the last mile. It's called "hitting the wall", and it's painful — in running and in business.

You learn your conditioning level by timing yourself over the course of months or even years. Your ability, stride length and mental toughness all play roles in determining your pace.

When you see running races on TV, the narrators often comment on the pace set by the leader. If it is too far above their personal best, the announcers will place bets on whether the runner has the mental toughness to keep it up at that pace.

In a similar way, the rush of adrenaline created by scanning emails, responding to urgent messages, reading exciting news or simply anticipating the day ahead creates a sense of lethargy and often despair before the day is over.

I believe that one of the secrets to success is to find your ideal pace for a successful workday.

Your pace includes the time of day you choose to carry out each priority, how long you spend doing it, and how quickly you tend to get things done.

Working too quickly can lead to costly errors. If you work too slowly, you miss deadlines or lose interest.

Your pace also depends on a variety of external factors, such as your workspace, colleagues, support, network of connections, product knowledge, communication skills, productivity, and habits.

When it comes to pacing yourself at work, the goal is not to become the fastest or to always finish first. The goal is to work at a pace that creates capacity for you to do more in less time.

Improving your pace is the key to working better, not harder.

The Perfect Day Framework

Think back to a "perfect day" in your business. If you perceive perfect to be an impossible standard, consider the things you most often attribute to make it a good, great, or even fantastic day!

Most people's perfect day includes something out of the ordinary that brings them joy.

It could be anything from a big sale to a friend's birth announcement, or a big win in some area of your life. A perfect day always has a cause for celebration.

A perfect day framework therefore, is simply setting yourself up for the biggest chance of having something to celebrate, every single day.

In order to accomplish something worth celebrating, three key variables need to be in place.

1. You need a focus for the day; focus brings energy.

2. You need to commit to that focus; commitment mobilizes your beliefs and actions.

3. Finally, you need to rise up, celebrate the win, and reset for the following day.

Let's explore each of these areas in more detail.

Focus

Focus is how you approach each day to give yourself the best chance of success, one priority at a time.

You will surprise yourself with how much more you can get done in a day when you give your undivided attention to the most important task at hand.

This is where you can get things done in half the time.

Focus is on a continuum. At times, we can focus for long periods without losing our concentration, intensity or drive.

My mother used to say that bombs could be going off and I would not lift my head out of a book. My husband calls me Belle (from *Beauty and the Beast*) because I always have my nose in a book!

The challenge for me is that I miss things. I miss important things people are saying or doing because I get so deeply absorbed in my own thoughts.

On the opposite end of the spectrum, we can also be completely unfocused. Our brains love to go down rabbit holes and chase shiny objects, oftentimes making it almost impossible to stay on the task at hand.

In his book, *Hyperfocus*, Chris Bailey describes these extremes as "Hyperfocus" and "Scatterfocus":

"The most recent neuroscientific research reveals that our brain has two powerful modes that can be unlocked when we use our attention effectively: a focused mode (hyperfocus), which is the foundation for being highly productive, and a creative mode (scatterfocus), which enables us to connect ideas in novel ways."

The perfect day embraces your need to be both scatterfocused and hyperfocused.

Every artist will tell you they thrive at the scattered end of the spectrum. They like to get messy before getting good. It's all part of the journey.

Another very important thing happens when you scatter your thoughts: you open your mind to infinite possibility. Often, the energy you need for the day lies in how creative you are in creating your day. One idea sparks another, and often uncovers a gem that motivates you to keep going!

In other words, sometimes, going down a rabbit hole helps you discover gold! You need to give yourself permission to do it in a controlled environment.

Hyperfocus is critical to eliminating distractions that are getting in the way of what you most need to accomplish.

Having a long to-do list of things you'll never get done eventually leads to a feeling of overwhelm. Compare that to three big priorities that you achieve every day. This hyperfocus leads to increased self-confidence and progress.

Here are a few ideas on how to leverage the spectrum of scatterfocus and hyperfocus.

Scatterfocus

 Start your day with scatterfocus. Be deliberate about getting ideas out of your head and onto paper. Don't limit yourself by diving into tasks. Enjoy the blank slate of the day. Use a whiteboard or a blank sheet of paper and create a mind map every morning of all the things you love and like to do in a day.

"Never start your day until you finish it on paper."

2 Scatterfocus to connect to your big goal. Creating the perfect day should always include a teaspoon of your big dream. After everything is out of your head, only proceed with those things that you can directly connect to your big goal.

3 Scatterfocus by looking for success all around you. Get there before you get there.

What would a superstar who is already where you want to be do with their day? When your habits and approach begin to align with those that are best class, you become world class.

Consider a professional athlete at the highest level.

When NBA superstar Kobe Bryant was at the peak of his career, he worked harder than anyone else. He was in elite condition, practices at an NBA finals level of intensity, and as careful about everything he ate. He also took a nap two hours before every game.

When our minor hockey and basketball coaches would insist our boys be at the rink two hours ahead of the game, only to sit in a tiny locker room with music blaring and no fresh air, I had my doubts. Is that really what a superstar would do?

When you are thinking about your approach, observe those who have already achieved the kind of success you seek, and model their behaviour.

"Success leaves clues."

~ Jim Rohn

Hyperfocus

1 Hyperfocus by prioritizing your tasks. The skill of converting a long list of tasks into three bigger priorities is a game-changer. In deep contrast to scatterfocus, consider 90 minutes of hyperfocus on a series of tasks that create a bigger result. It is similar to the way a surgeon considers a surgery.

"People assume that a surgeon's skill is primarily in the precision and steadiness of his or her hands. While there's some truth to that, the true gift of a surgeon is the ability to single-mindedly focus on one person and complete a series of tasks over the course of many hours,"

~ Cynthia Kobu, PhD

2 Gamify it. When you look at your long task list, the game is to find tasks and lump them together.

The game is to condense tasks into bigger priorities so you make progress. The challenge is to start tracking how much you can get done in a day. You will start to pick up the pace, and get better and better at doing similar tasks in batches to reduce the cost of switching tasks.

3   Hyperfocus through strict time slots. Set times for recess, socializing, and an end of the day celebration. Remember in school when that recess bell rang you got an instant jolt of joy! Playtime, talking time, and snack time. After school we had playdates and sports.

As adults, we lose the ability to do for ourselves what we were conditioned to do in school; take organized breaks, socialize, and get outside — even in the pouring rain and snow.

During the pandemic, one of the leading causes of depression was that people were no longer getting out the way they were used to. Days and weeks would go by without a routine walk around the block.

4   Hyperfocus by shutting down all notifications. Interruptions are the enemy of focus. In fact, research shows that we lose 40 per cent of our productivity switching tasks.

Psychologists suggest likening your job to choreography or air-traffic control, noting that in these operations, as in others, mental overload can result in catastrophe.

In her article in *Psychology Today*, Susan Weinschenk explains that there is no such thing as multitasking.

We actually can only work on one thing at a time so we're actually switching tasks, which is where the greatest amount of productivity is lost.

We no longer people-watch in grocery lines or in a doctor's office. We dive into phones because we think doing so will ease the pain of not having something stimulating to focus on.

Therefore, at the first hint of the mundane or boring in our daily tasks, we crave the quick hit of social media.

The other day, I was coaching a client. Her goals were big and her ability to work hard was impressive. Yet, throughout the entire conversation, we had on-hold music playing in the background.

Her phone went off, we paused while she took a pocket-call. It went off again. This time, slightly embarrassed, she looked at the number. It was a girlfriend calling to ask about dinner. She would call her back.

When I followed up on her homework, she admitted she was too busy to get to it. She'd developed a habit of snorkeling through her day rather than scuba diving to get to the heart of what was holding her back.

90-Minute Zones

The second key element of focus is to put work into 90-minute zones of productivity. As human beings, we are deeply influenced by the type of work and the energy required to complete it. Jim Loehr and Tony Schwartz, authors of The Power of Full Engagement, stress, "Energy, not time, is the fundamental currency of high performance".

Zones of productivity take into consideration your energy as it relates to the series of tasks you must move through.

Consider the energy required to achieve your goals. There are three unique energy zones: the zones of creativity, connection, and construction.

Zone of Creativity

This zone is where you focus on becoming you! It's the best version of yourself. You invest time setting up your day, working on a skill, or working on your business.

Planning, creating, dreaming, and scheming all happen in your zone of creativity.

Typically, the time to enter this zone is first thing in the morning or last thing in your day. However, long walks in the middle of the day, doodling while listening to a webinar, or listening to a highly inspirational speaker can all spark creativity.

Zone of Connection

This zone involves connecting and communicating with others. This activity gives extroverts energy. For introverts, it might take away energy.

An example of this is sales calls. If you struggle with reaching out and connecting with clients proactively, this zone needs to be scheduled to the peak of your day.

Find a time when both your energy and your productive outcomes have the highest chance of colliding. Your energy might be highest first thing in the morning, but your chances of connecting with people then is low.

Zone of Construction

This is the zone of putting your brain to work for longer periods of time. This is where concentration and attention to detail are essential. Ultimately, this is where you create your customer service wow.

This is where you perform the surgery.

Pulling It All Together and Putting It in Your Calendar

- When do you have the best energy for putting your intelligence into high gear?

- When do you have the energy required to communicate with others?

- When is your best creative time?

A 10X strategy is to pay attention to similar types of tasks, group them together in a way that makes sense, and, finally, to schedule them at a recurring time in your calendar that matches your best energy.

Commit

Now the work begins. At this point, you have constructed your do list in order to work on your key priorities that will make the biggest impact towards achieving your goals. The commit stage is the epitome of choosing what to do and what to do next.

There are many schools of thought on choosing your next move. The one that inspires me the most is by Gary Keller. He recommend choosing the one thing that is going to create the biggest impact on your long-term goals. *"What's the one thing, such that by doing it, makes everything else easier or unnecessary?", he asks.*

The "one thing" theory is a theory about making good decisions in your business.

Your next move can be the biggest decision of your life.

Committing to one thing sounds simple but it is profound. It requires choosing the next best thing, and doing it, no matter what.

There are two traps that we fall into when committing.

The first is choosing a priority that is way too big. Marketing or social media are not tasks, they are strategies. Big topics like these hang over us, building up pressure over time.

The other is doing busy work that is not moving the needle: agonizing over the wording of an email, or sitting pondering what to say on a social media post. Or worse — and I am guilty of this — creating the post and not sending it!

Every day, commit to five things that are significant enough to move the needle in your business.

The Rule of Five

Much has been written about how many priorities is the right amount to get things done. Jim Collins, author of Good to Great, suggests, "If you have more than three priorities, you have none".

A priority is a significant task that takes you towards your goal.

What I have learned with the help of Robin Sharma, author of The 5AM Club, is to set a blueprint for my perfect day with just the right number of tasks on the list to push me a little harder than I'm comfortable with, yet not enough to burden me with a long list of things to complete.

I've settled on the rule of five. Here's how it works.

If you are a list maker, your list may start out as 20 different items. Take the time to group them into no more than five bigger tasks.

This one action of scatterfocusing the big list and narrowing it into a condensed set of actions is a 10X productivity transformation.

Completing five sets of high-impact activities every day has a compounding impact. It forces you to think about the big picture and get everything out of your head and onto paper.

Narrowing the bigger list by both grouping like activities and deleting meaningless distractions provides both clarity and a realistic roadmap to getting things done.

Let's consider the math on the five-item rule. If you had 20 things on your to-do list, chances are, you would complete the top 5 on the list (or 20 per cent).

By condensing your list down from 20 tasks to 5 priorities, you can achieve 4 out of 5 tasks daily, completing 80 per cent of your tasks instead of 20 per cent! It has a profound compound effect.

James Clear states: "If you get one per cent better each day for one year, you'll end up thirty-seven times better by the time you're done".

Grouping tasks into priorities, rather than taking them on one task at a time, may be the most significant productivity improvement you can make in your business.

Reset

The final framework for the perfect day blueprint is to reset. Resetting is the act of recognizing that you've done all you can do to make this day what it was — good, bad, or mediocre.

It includes reviewing what you accomplished, rising up and celebrating the wins, and acknowledging what needs to be on the list for the next day.

Each day is the day we make it.

We are 100 per cent responsible for the day we've experienced. We may not be accountable for all that happens to us, but we are responsible for how we respond to it.

Often, we start out with the best intentions, but the day explodes, and we lose track of what we set out to do in the first place.

That is completely normal and understandable — sometimes we need to yield to urgent requests or respond to unexpected demands from customers — but if it happens every day, it leads to burnout.

Starting the day knowing that at the end of the day you are accountable to yourself changes the way you approach the work.

Imagine your own awards ceremony.

When you write out your intentions for the day, think about how it will feel at the end of the day when you get to celebrate yourself.

I use *The Five Minute Journal,* recommended to me by a colleague. The power of this journal is that not only does it capture gratitude and intentions, but it also forces you to evaluate what you achieved.

- What are three things I am grateful for?

- What would make today great?

- What is my daily affirmation ("I am...")?

- Name three amazing things that happened today.

- How could I have made today even better?

The last two are critical to the concept of resetting.

The ritual of evaluating progress every day and resetting for the next day creates a sense of small wins and perpetual momentum in your business.

The practice of ticks in boxes is the universal language of resetting. The difference between checking off boxes and the practice of resetting is the framework of focusing, committing, and resetting.

Each day, you set aside no more than five big priorities for the day and commit to the one thing that would propel you forward.

When you reset, consider what you got done, and why it matters.

For example, if you know you need to expand your connections with your database and for the past week but you've been putting it off, you must examine the deeper root cause of the delay.

Busyness is the enemy of progress and a symptom of procrastination.

Five Actions for the Day — Only Move It Twice

Each day, set up your perfect day with five actions for the day.

At the end of the day, you get the satisfaction of reviewing the list, and acknowledging your achievements. Most days, there will be one or two things that don't get done... that's okay!

The secret is to only allow yourself to move the unfinished task twice.

If you have to move it a third time, there is something else going on.

Either delete if from the list, or get it done and out of the way.

The perfect day blueprint includes a focus for the day. That focus is a reminder of what matters most. It's the ideal time to consider what you need to do in this moment to bring your vision one step closer to becoming a reality.

Once the day is in focus, it's time to commit to the group of activities that will make the biggest difference towards achieving your goal. The art of creating a do list from a to-do list is a high-impact 10X strategy.

Finally, measuring progress and celebrating your journey is the art of rising up.

This beautiful verse poem by Emily Dickinson is my inspiration for rising each and every day.

"We never know how high we are
Till we are called to rise;
And then, if we are true to plan,
Our statures touch the skies"

Chapter Summary
10X Impact — Part Two
Executing the Dream

- Once you notice your natural rhythms, and you align those rhythms with your purpose, along with the work that needs to get done to fulfil it, a new world of productivity opens up to you.

- The approach *is* the work.

- If the perfect day is a cake recipe, the tasks and priorities are the ingredients and method, and the big goal is the cake!

- Priorities are groups of tasks that, when done consistently, will make the biggest impact on your business.

- Priorities allow you to create the do list instead of the to-do list.

- When it comes to pacing yourself at work, the goal is not to become the fastest or to always finish first. The goal is to work at a pace that creates capacity for you to do more in less time.

- The perfect day embraces your need to be both scatterfocused and hyperfocused.

- Focus is how you approach each day to give yourself the best chance of success, one priority at a time.

- There are three unique energy zones: creativity, connection, and construction.

- Every day, commit to five things that are significant enough to move the needle in your business.

- Narrowing the bigger list by grouping like activities and deleting meaningless distractions provides clarity and a realistic roadmap to getting things done.

- The ritual of evaluating progress every day and resetting for the next day creates a sense of small wins and perpetual momentum in your business.

Points to Ponder

- What natural rhythms of energy do you pay attention to when creating your calendar?

- How might scheduling work according to the energy it requires improve your productivity?

- How do you feel after you get everything out of your head and onto paper (scatterfocus)?

- Narrow all of your activities down to five priorities. How does narrowing your focus make you feel? What did you eliminate and what types of activities did you group together?

- Design your perfect day by committing to five actions every day for fourteen days.

- What percentage of your list do you think will get done when you have 20 items compared to 5 priorities in a single day?

- How do you celebrate each day?

Part Four

10X Leadership

Chapter 9

10X Together: How to Engage a Superstar Team

"If you want to go fast, go alone.
If you want to go far, go together."

~ African proverb.

If you want to 10X your travel business, you simply will not get there alone.

Whether you're a host, own a large agency, or are an independent travel advisor hoping to bring others under your wing, 10X together is about putting the goals of others ahead of your own.

Note: if you are an independent travel agent, you may skip this chapter. However, the principals of teamwork are for everyone. You may find it useful to understand how important being part of a winning team is to your individual success.

Step One: Put Your Team First

The first step of growing your team is making their goals as important or more important than your own.

From day one, consider adding to your team, not as a means to 10X your business, but as a way to help others become ten times better at achieving their dreams.

One of the most common roadblocks to recruitment I hear is that "I tried that, and it was a complete disaster" or, "I can't find anyone who is as committed as I am".

Megan, a high-producing independent agent, had hit the ceiling at almost two million in personal sales. She was exhausted and couldn't keep up with the demand for her time and attention.

She tried to bring on an independent contractor to take on some of her clients. Unfortunately, it ended in complete frustration. The contractor left her high and dry. She scrambled to cover all of the clients who were needing help, on top of her own clients.

She was very reluctant to consider growing her team ever again.

Megan had the common roadblock of high standards that were not being met. This is completely understandable as the whole point of becoming 10X better is to become "Best in the world".

When I asked Megan how much time she had taken to onboard her new-hire, she admitted that it probably wasn't enough.

When I asked about her process for creating lifelong customers, she realized she hadn't really thought about it. It was "in her head".

She had set aside time on an ad hoc basis, but didn't have a non-negotiable block of time in her calendar or a structured approach to the key skill of transferring customer service knowledge.

The key takeaway? Get it out of your head!

When adding to your team, ensure you have dedicated, non-negotiable time in your calendar.

One of the best recruiters in the industry, who adds thirty to forty ICs per month, shared his best tip:

"The minute I bring someone on, I share my 12-week onboarding plan, complete with thirty-minute weekly meeting every Friday. I never cancel. If they cancel, I chase them until we have the meeting."

Secondly, have a documented, step-by-step checklist of how things are done to your high standards.

Remember: 10X doesn't happen overnight but it is a daily endeavour.

Step Two: Delegate Your Own Clients

Another client, Tracy, has a small team. However, she is by far the largest producer on her team.

"I've tried delegating my clients but they won't move. They only want to deal with me!"

Every person who has ever moved from one level of success to another has faced the challenge of people who did not want to lose them in the role they were in.

Yet, if you stay where you are, you are limiting the impact you can make on others in the world.

Take, for example, the proprietor of my hair salon, Tara. I started as her client years ago. She worked miracles on my hair and the experience was like visiting a good friend.

She became wildly popular and it was getting more and more difficult to find an appointment time. She had reached the ceiling of time and the amount she could earn.

Tara recognized the challenge, and at the same time was really excited about growing her small business. She wanted to be the go-to salon in the community.

Her solution was to delegate 100 per cent of her clients to her team. She hired a rockstar salon host (receptionist) to communicate the message of how things were changing for the better, and added five more stylists.

Instead of cutting hair, Tara focused on client satisfaction through her team.

She spent the first ten minutes of every appointment on the consultation. She mingled among clients and saw to it that everything was executed according to her high standards. Not one person left the salon until she'd given the Tara Seal of Approval.

Watching her coach and encourage her team was seeing a whole new talent come to life.

As a client, I was thrilled for her. She'd found a new way to do what she loved, and now she is passing her unique gifts on to her team.

Learn from Tara's example. Tarafound joy in her new found skills of leader, coach, and cheerleader.

The key takeaway? To grow 10X together is an important leap from doing to leading.

Step 3: Becoming a 10X Leader Through Deep Empathy and Engagement.

Leadership is hard. It can also be the most fulfilling thing you'll ever do.

These past two years have been a series of extreme highs and lows. Staying in front of this pandemic has been particularly challenging for those who are doing their best to lead others through it.

You lack certainty; you don't even know the right words to say. This leaves you feeling helpless and frustrated.

For most leaders, particularly those focused on high performance, engagement is the most enduring goal on the list.

Show me a successful entrepreneur and I'll show you a dedicated, enthusiastic, and engaged team.

Yet, even the best among you struggles to keep the entire team engaged.

You are often resigned to the timeless 80/20 principal. Eighty percent of your results come from 20 per cent of your team.

Then, when your superstars take a hit, it rocks their world.

One new trend I've noticed through the pandemic is that, rather than losing the low producers, our superstars who had the biggest client lists took the biggest hits because they suffered the most cancellations. The result is that good people are leaving!

In other words, the bigger they are, the harder they fall! Some irreversibly so. We've lost too many good advisors to count!

The mistake most leaders make is trying old strategies to engage a newly enlightened travel community. Travel advisors are tougher, more realistic, and less willing to work for nothing anymore.

Sometimes, team members move slowly up or down, depending on the uncertainty of the day. Other times, they remain stuck at a point in their engagement. If they flounder for too long or fail to form a new set of behaviours, they cannot continue.

The solution to growing 10X together, is deep empathy. It means meeting team members where they are at and helping them rise above it.

The following is an empathy roadmap to highlight the stages of team engagement.

10X Together Empathy Roadmap

How I am	How I Feel	Impact
Flourishing	Sought After	10X
Focused	Confident	5X
Forming	In Control	1X
Floundering	Frustrated	- 5X
Falling	I'm done!	- 10X

Falling

"I'm done", she announced flatly. Then, she repeated it three times for emphasis. Leanne is an award-winning travel advisor and has been the top producer for many years for her travel organization.

Falling is an ongoing state that can happen to the best and the least of us. We are all prone to this kind of devastation.

It can happen once, or it can be a gradual degradation of your time and energy.

In the falling stage, there is no end to the bad news. You can no longer ignore what you feel is the universe asking you, "Why do you stay?" — it feels like mockery.

As one advisor said to me, "I don't want to be made to feel foolish for staying this long".

The worst part of falling is that you would never wish it on anyone, and when it happens to your best people you feel helpless and angry for them.

The real problem? There's nothing to fear but fear itself, and that's not nothing! The fear is real, and the fear is paralysing.

The Solution

When a team member is in the falling stage, the solution is to acknowledge it, and recognize their value.

Acknowledge that you see them and accept them for where they are at. Appreciate that where they are is real to them. Recognize and appreciate that they have endured the journey.

In the falling stage, no amount of convincing will work. The solution to falling is not to stand them back up again, but to break their fall through acceptance.

Sometimes, "I see you, I hear you, I feel your pain" is all anyone needs to hear. Let them know they will be accepted back in the game, when the time is right.

Floundering

In the floundering stage, advisors have one foot in and one foot out. The passion for the business is there but it is so dim, you can barely see the flame.

The temptation is to keep giving them instructions or ideas to try. Your best attempts to get them to act only make matters worse. It's like building a fire; if you add wood too quickly, the flame will completely go out.

The reason people vacillate or fail to execute good ideas is largely based on fear.

Fear of failure is part of it. Perhaps they lack skill or experience. What if they try what you're asking of them, and it backfires?

There is also the fear of success.

What if they do win more customers, grow bigger, and grow more noticeable? Will they be able to handle the success?

I love this quote from *The Life of Pi.*

"Fear is life's only true opponent."

The erosion of confidence and conviction through all types of fear is at the heart of the floundering stage.

The Solution

When you're floundering, it's time to re-frame the opportunity. The key to addressing fear is to create certainty in everything you know to be true. For example,

1. There is a better future ahead. In fact, the future of travel will be much better, not despite the pandemic, but because of it. The comeback is not better than the setback. The comeback is IN the setback.

    The silver lining is the reminder that life is precious, and that meaningful experiences matter. Travel falls into the bigger bucket of meaningful experiences.

    Helping people delight in the experience of travel will be the compass for navigating our way back.

2. Good travel advisors are in hot demand.

    Many industries are dealing with massive digital disruption since the pandemic hit. Online ordering, Instacart, Insta — everything!

    Travel is heading in the opposite direction.

We've already undergone a digital disruption. We've been on the brink of possible extinction as a travel advisor community.

There is so much evidence of why now, more than ever, using a travel agent is a good decision.

The benefit to your advisors is that for the first time in a very long time, they will be in the driver's seat of demand.

The key is to focus on helping them communicate their value.

③ There is a pent-up demand of unused vacation days and dollars.

The consumer has missed out on so many lived experiences. They are ready to make up for lost time. The average spend will be dramatically higher, therefore so will the earning opportunity.

Once you re-frame the opportunity that addresses the root cause of fear, the advisor can see a brighter future ahead with themselves in it.

The next stage is to help your advisors form, focus, and flourish with this new, enlightened understanding in mind.

Forming

In this stage, advisors are developing the confidence and conviction to move forward.

They are forming a new vision for their business and taking the right actions to bring their business to life.

You might say they have caught fire! The flames are growing, but their fire is still vulnerable to heavy rain and wind; a gust in the wrong direction may still extinguish it. This pandemic has been the source of many such gusts and put out many little fires.

The Solution

The solution in the forming stage is to focus on systems. The more you can remove unnecessary steps, and help advisors focus on the key actions that will create a customer, the faster they will flourish.

In the next chapter, we'll review a 10X framework which will allow you to form a system of high performance.

Focused

In this stage, there are clear goals and a detailed plan. The plan is well executed and gets better over time.

The difference between forming and focused is that focused advisors have a system for attracting, servicing, and keeping customers.

These advisors are on a steady climb towards a higher level of achievement. They have their goals clearly in place, and there is clear evidence of progress.

Focused advisors are not afraid to fail. They see setbacks as a chance to learn and get better next time.

The Solution

In the higher stages of an advisor's path to success, you will see less work creating greater results. This advisor has let go of trying to be all things to all people.

They are clear on what and who to say no to, to make room for a bigger yes.

Your role as a leader is to have their back. Giving advisors permission to say no can be hard, especially when you are focused on regaining your financial positioning.

Yet, in the long run, the most important element of leading a high-producing team is to empower your advisors to choose who they will work with.

Flourishing

"I am the go-to advisor in my community." "She's the one!"

They are the advisor most customers are seeking.

Flourishing advisors are uniquely positioned for repeat clients, advocacy and referrals. They are known by others for their expertise and are easy to recommend.

The key to this stage is that the dollars per client are going up and the time taken to produce those dollars is going down.

Better customers, bigger transactions, and more repeat and referral customers are the hallmarks of a flourishing advisor.

Solution
Staying in the flourishing stage is a lofty yet attainable goal.

Flourishing advisors have a very high level of repeat and referral clients. They do less work to achieve better results. They follow a system of creating customers for life.

The 10X Together Strategy
The 10X together strategy is simple.

Go deeper with your current team so that you are not overly reliant on a few key producers.

A word of caution. 10X together may be simple, but it is not a quick fix.

It requires a long-range growth mindset that focuses on getting better, not bigger. In other words, it requires you to recognize the behaviours you seek, not the results.

It means meeting people where they are by using the empathy roadmap. You cannot rush relationship building or human connections.

However, the methodology is quite simple. A few small changes and you can see the possibilities of a total transformation of your leadership in a very short period of time.

The Five Rules of Becoming 10X Together

Better always comes before bigger. When you become a better leader, incredible things are just around the corner. There are five rules of engagement.

Better Skills

Better leadership skills are the gateway to high performance. In the same way that an advisor is powerless without product knowledge and sales skills, a leader is lost without one-on-one communication skills.

Tip: Invest at least part of every single day learning how to effectively communicate, influence, engage, and help people WANT to be accountable to their goals.

Better Connections

You are the company you keep. When you stay within the circle you already know, you limit your ability to grow. Everything you need is slightly outside your comfort zone, especially when it comes to networking.

Tip: Seek out leaders you admire. Find people who already have a thriving and engaged team, and follow their path.

Better Alignment with Advisors

When I ask most leaders why they entered the travel industry, the answer involves their passion. Passion for travel, passion for what they sell, passion for the industry. When I ask why they stay, the answer is always the same: "I stay because of my team". You stay because of the people who have been loyal to you and seek your leadership.

Setting a goal for better alignment with advisors is about setting the bar around your core values. For example,

- **Trust:** If you want if you want a trusting team, be trustworthy.

- **Dedication:** If you want a dedicated team, be dedicated to your team first.

- **Teamwork:** If you want a loyal team, consider what teamwork means to you. Does it mean loyal to you or does it mean loyal to the values you represent? If you want a loyal team, live your values.

Better Pay

For a long time, the industry has almost apologized for the lower levels of pay. The joy of the job, the perks, and the passion seemed to be an excuse for not talking about the money. A wise person told me, "If you want to make more money, you need to talk about the money".

Tip: You need a business that is fun, fulfilling, and financially rewarding. Two out of three is not enough.

Better Balance

10X my team is about growing ten times better in half the time. The balance you seek is at the crossroads of time and energy. You cannot manage time, but you can and should manage your energy.

Tip: High performance is dependent on doing the right things at the right times, based on your energy.

This is critical when it comes to meeting your people. If you want to do your best work with your people, find the right time and bring the right energy.

Chapter Summary
10X Together

- For most leaders, particularly those focused on high performance, engagement is the most enduring goal on the list.

- You are often resigned to the timeless 80/20 principle, whereby 80 per cent of your results come from 20 per cent of your team.

- The solution to advisor attraction and engagement is to meet advisors where they are at and help them rise above it.

- Falling advisors need to be seen and accepted for where they are at.

- Floundering advisors require you to re-frame the opportunity.

- Forming advisors have a system to efficiently and effectively create customers.

- Flourishing advisors are the go-to advisors for a strong community of customers.

- 10X my team is a strategy for going deeper with your current team so that you are not overly reliant on a few key producers.

- Better always comes before bigger. When you become a better leader, incredible things are just around the corner.

Conclusion

The 10X approach to dreaming, growing, and rebuilding your business is not about working harder. It's about thinking bigger and getting better.

The 10X lens is a handy tool for using on a daily basis in your business. The first question to ask yourself is, "Am I 10X Ready?". That means ensuring you have the capacity to add a new goal to your plate.

If the answer is yes, the next step is to evaluate every task on the list. It's a simple yes or no question.

Does doing this next step take me closer to my goal? If yes, then it becomes a matter of deciding which is the most important next step.

Another vital consideration is what you will say no to. Using your 10X lens, what are the things you're doing that are no longer needed? You might ask, will this action attract or retain my ideal customers? So much of what we did prior to the pandemic was busy work, but was it all necessary work?

In a post pandemic era, where everything takes a little longer and has more meaning, we can't afford to do things that don't contribute to creating a customer.

Get tough on what you say no to in order to leave room for a more important yes!

Finally, the 10X lens is important for creating a craftsman approach to becoming best in the world at what you do. When you stop trying to be all things to all people, you can focus on the skills you need to be best in the world for the customers you care about.

10X My Travel Business, doing ten times better in half the time, requires a new way of thinking. The framework necessary for 10X growth lies in the following four key areas.

- **Purpose.** You've come this far and stayed engaged with an industry that has been through such a devastating set back. It's important, if not essential, that you examine why you started the business in the first place, and why you stay.

   When you share your purpose with others, it allows you to deliver an experience that has far more meaning than just another trip. In a post-pandemic era, there is no such thing as a simple getaway.

Travel carries so much more meaning than that. It's the perfect opportunity to examine your own motives. Your purpose is what sets you apart.

- **People.** There is no doubt that the comeback is going to be massive. There will be an abundance of customers looking for help. There is almost a desperation to helping travelers navigate the complexities of travel. It's the perfect time to decide on the kind of customers that light you up!

- **Process**. Everything is going to take a little longer. There is so much change that nothing feels routine anymore. Therefore, to make progress without losing your way, you need to do less. Your process needs to find ways to simplify and systemize delivering a vacation experience.

- **Performance.** Traditional goalsetting was all about the numbers. 10X performance is about so much more. It's a goal for not only how big your business will be, but how you will feel when you are operating at maximum capacity. Your mojo is a precious resource. Measuring and having a plan for what brings you joy is all part of a new 10X approach.

Now that you've examined the four pillars of a 10X framework, you must consider the strategies for achieving a 10X travel business. There are four key strategies to becoming 10X better in half the time.

10X Connection: Connection Is Currency

Strategy #1

Connection means growing customer relationships through meaningful, frequent, and consistent actions. It involves creating a system for segmenting and converting customers for life.

The strength of your connection is powerful in determining your success. The relationship you have with your database is a leading indicator of not only how big you can grow, but the amount of effort it will take to achieve it.

The better the relationships you have, the easier it will be to build your business for the future.

There are three segments of your connections — each with their own strategies for strengthening the return on your investment.

- **Circle of Influence**
  They are not known to you yet, but they are similar to those you are already familiar with and consider ideal. The action here is to build your visibility and awareness within this segment.

- **Circle of Significance**
  These customers are in a relationship with you. The goal is to deepen the bond and to keep adding and releasing based on their propensity for future travel.

- **Circle of Advocacy**
  These ideal customers are your raving fans. They wouldn't think of traveling without you and they bring others to you.

10X Conversion: The Art of Creating a High-Value Customer

Strategy #2:
Conversion: To create a steady stream of high-value customers through customer attraction, retention, and ongoing skilling up.

Customer attraction is the sum of the activities that put you in the path of your ideal customer. It includes marketing, social media, your website, your online presence, newsletters, warm touchpoints, and most importantly calling.

Customer retention is your ability to convert customers into customers for life. Your ability to ask better questions, narrow the list of options, and to go above and beyond is critical, not just to the vacation at hand; it also ensures that a good customer is a repeat customer.

Skilling up is more than learning a new skill. It's actually how to learn faster and more effectively in order to become the best in the industry at what you do.

These three areas make up the strategy of conversion.

10X Commercial: Increasing Your Financial Wellbeing

Strategy #3

To be commercial is to increase revenue by helping customers buy well, by upselling, and by implementing service fees. It means improving sales through urgency, psychology, formality and fluency.

If there is one aspect of the travel industry that stands out as being different than prior to the pandemic, it is the clarity around becoming financially viable. With each booking taking longer and the unprecedented demand for knowledge and advice, the industry is positioned well for earning more money.

The importance of asking better questions and helping customers buy their own elevated experiences is a terrific strategy for earning more commission.

Charging fees is new for some advisors. Whether you charge a fee or not, the critical line in the sand is not giving away your very hard-earned advice for free. Stay in the why before they buy!

10X Impact: From Transactional to Transformational

Strategy #4

Making an impact through creating life-changing travel experiences for clients.

This journey has been a long one. We are on the foothills of Comeback Mountain. As we head up this mountain, the goal is to reach the highest heights in the fewest steps.

More importantly, the goal is to make a positive impact in the world through the service we provide. Helping the world start traveling again is a noble cause.

The journey forward depends on deepening the meaning of our actions from transactional to transformational.

Now that we have an understanding of the foundation of a 10X travel business, and the strategies necessary to achieve it, we need a systematic approach to high achievement.

The 10X success blueprint is a step-by-step approach to getting what you want, without losing your way.

It starts with a clear and compelling vision. It encompasses all the trimming, like a motion picture of your dreams.

Your big word encompasses the meaning behind what you want to achieve with your travel business. Your priorities are the big ideas captured in a specific way so that getting things done is clear and measurable.

A big part of the perfect day blueprint is to identify the gaps in skills and habits. The reason for this is that a small daily effort over time adds up to a remarkable transformation.

Your perfect day is a combination of leveraging time and managing energy. Matching the activities that will take you towards your goal with the right energy zone makes a big difference to your results.

Scheduling your priorities into the calendar is key. If something is important enough to be a priority, there shouldn't be more than a day or two toes by before some small effort takes place.

The perfect day is based on making a decision. Committing to a plan for the day and getting it done! At the end of every day, take time to celebrate the wins of the day, and rise!

Congratulations, you've got everything you need to build a travel business that is ten times better in half the time! I look forward to seeing you on Comeback Mountain!

About Geraldine Ree

Geraldine is the bestselling author of Flying Colours and 10X My Travel Business. She is an accomplished industry leader, keynote speaker, and mentor. She is known for sharing rich insights that shift your thinking and create game-changing productivity strategies for audiences and clients alike.

What's unique about Geraldine is that she's held every seat at the table. In fact, she says, no matter what role you have in the travel industry,

"I've walked a mile in your shoes, and I've worn every shoe in the closet!"

She began selling corporate travel "door to door" for Wardair. It was here she learned the importance of a good list, persistence, and getting past no!

Next, Geraldine spent 17 years leading field sales teams at Princess Cruises. Never in a million years would she have predicted how valuable learning how to thrive remotely would pay off during the Covid years.

When Geraldine joined the leadership team of Expedia Cruises, she earned her stripes in both entrepreneurship and advanced learning. Tasked with helping hundreds of Franchise Owners and thousands of ICs who were brand new to the industry learn, she developed a keen sense of what mattered most and what didn't matter at all.

After close to three decades of working with travel business owners, Geraldine caught the business building bug and made the leap to become an entrepreneur.

In an ironic twist, despite almost three decades of unprecedented, good times in the travel industry, it's these past two years of pushing through the hardship to build a business she loves, that inspires her the most.

Today Geraldine works with travel agents, owners, suppliers, and industry leaders to help them achieve the life they've always wanted, within an industry that, despite all its challenges, they never want to leave!

Geraldine lives in White Rock, BC, with her husband Cam, and her faithful four-legged companion, Blueberry. She is currently working on her third book, Becoming Us—lessons in leading the travel industry forward.

Connect With Me

There are a few ways to connect with me!

1.   **Subscribe to my newsletters! I write two blogs.**
   - The Shift Room – Exclusively for Travel Advisors
   - On Leadership – Helping Leaders 10X Together
   Sign up at www.Geraldineree.com

2.   **Elevate Mentorship**
   Elevate Mentorship is for high-achieving leaders who want to increase the impact of their work. The purpose is to help you find your unique ability and to leverage it as a guiding light.

   We will move through a step-by-step process to getting everything you want.

   If you're like most of the leaders I work with, figuring out exactly what you want is a big part of the journey. It doesn't always happen overnight. Growing and developing takes time, and it takes someone with experience and expertise to come along side you. Let's do it together!

3. **Supplier Team Leadership – The Power of Me, to We, to Us**
    I help high-performing field sales teams adapt, engage, and capture the vastly evolved B-to-B market. This content can be delivered in a full-day workshop or ongoing through a series of sessions.

    - The Power of Me – Mindset, Method, and Mastery
    - The Power of We – How to Find, Engage, and Grow with the New Travel Advisor
    - The Power of Us – How to build your own community in a new travel era.

4. **Keynotes**
    I offer a variety of keynotes and workshops that can be customized to your Conference themes. Here are a few recent examples.

    - Looking Up: What's Changed, What's Coming, What's Next
    - 10X My Travel Business: Ten Times Better in Half the Time
    - 10X Together: Comeback Better, Together: How to Lead a Team of Superstars
    - Changing the Game of Niches: It's Not What You Think!

5. **Flying Colours Academy**
   This is a 12-week facilitated program that includes online learning, homework, and shared experiences. If you're ready to 10X your business, this is the program for you! I help high-achieving travel advisors build the business of their dreams, without losing their way.

   Join me on this journey of unpacking high achievement as I work with like-minded people to achieve their 10X Goals!

   Find out more at **www.geraldineree.com** or email **geraldine@geraldineree.com**

Made in the USA
Las Vegas, NV
21 October 2023

79458031R00157